Ideas and Options
in
English for Specific Purposes

ESL & Applied Linguistics Professional Series
Eli Hinkel, Series Editor

Ideas and Options
in
English for Specific Purposes

Helen Basturkmen
The University of Auckland

Routledge
Taylor & Francis Group

NEW YORK AND LONDON

First published by
Lawrence Erlbaum Associates, Inc., Publishers
10 Industrial Avenue
Mahwah, New Jersey 07430
www.erlbaum.com

Transferred to Digital Printing 2009 by Routledge
270 Madison Ave, New York NY 10016
2 Park Square, Milton Park, Abingdon, Oxon, OX14 4RN

Cover design by Kathryn Houghtaling Lacey

Library of Congress Cataloging-in-Publication Data

Basturkmen, Helen.
    Ideas and options in English for specific purposes / Helen Basturkmen
       p.   cm.
    Includes bibliographical references and index.
    ISBN 0–8058–4417–1 — ISBN 0–8058–4418–X (pbk.)
    1. English language—Study and teaching (Higher)—Foreign
speakers. 2. English language—Business English—Study and teaching
(Higher) 3. English language—Technical English—Study and teaching
(Higher) I. Title.
PE1128.A2.B317 2005
428'.0071—dc22   2005047285

Contents

Part III: General

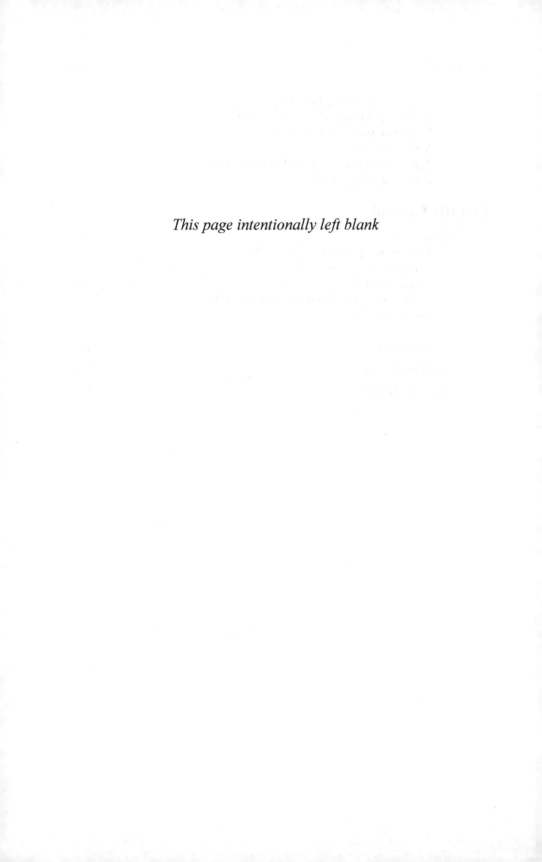

This page intentionally left blank

Preface

This is a book about different approaches to English for Specific Purposes (ESP). Much of the literature in ESP to date has focused on case-by-case descriptions of individual teaching or research projects. It has also focused on practical aspects, such as course and materials design (Dudley-Evans & St. John, 1998). The purpose of this book is to go beyond individual cases and practices to examine the approaches and the ideas on which they are based. The book does not seek to promote any one approach but to identify and illustrate the approaches in evidence today. The work addresses questions such as: What types of ESP teaching are practiced? What are the alternatives in ESP course design and what ideas about language and learning are they based on? What different roles can ESP teaching play? What kinds of research are carried out into the communicative practices of professional, academic, and workplace groups? How are theories from second language acquisition (SLA) reflected in ESP? What links are there between the emergence of a sociopolitical awareness in education and ESP?

This book is primarily geared toward the interests of participants on graduate-level TESOL teacher education courses. It serves as a basis for examination of theories and the links between them and practice and research in ESP. It aims to encourage readers to adopt an analytical stance toward the field, to identify the approaches in ESP today and the ideas driving them.

This is a book about ideas—the different views of language, learning, and teaching in ESP. However, it is not a book about ideas in the abstract. The main emphasis of the book is on the links between theory and ESP teaching and research. Ideas from linguistics, sociolinguistics, education, SLA, and social theories are described. Links are then made between them and ESP course designs, instructional materials, and research projects. Thus the work moves back and forth between description of theories, teaching practice, and research.

ESP is taught in many different countries and contexts. Recognizing this, the book draws on a wide range of examples of teaching practice and research from around the world and from different branches of ESP, including English for Academic Purposes (EAP), English for Professional Purposes (EPP), and English for Vocational Purposes (EVP).

OVERVIEW

The book has three parts. Part I introduces the book's approach to description of ESP and the framework used to investigate ESP. Chapter 1 identifies gaps in the current literature on ESP. Chapter 2 outlines the approach to description of ESP used in the book. Chapter 3 examines general issues in ESP course design.

Part II examines ideas of language, learning, and teaching in ESP. Chapters 4 and 5 are concerned with the types of language descriptions used in ESP. Chapter 4 examines descriptions of language systems and chapter 5 examines descriptions of language use. Chapter 6 illustrates ESP course and research designs that combine different descriptions. Chapters 7 and 8 examine ideas of learning in relation to ESP. Chapter 7 explores ideas about conditions needed for learning and chapter 8 explores ideas about how learning occurs in ESP in relation to the literature on second language acquisition. Chapters 9 and 10 discuss teaching. Chapter 9 examines options in ESP methodology. Chapter 10 investigates ESP teaching objectives. Recent years have seen a growing awareness of the sociopolitical implications of ESP teaching. Criticisms have been voiced that ESP is often a force for accommodation rather than change, and calls have been made for a critical ESP (Benesch, 2001). Chapter 10 explores conventional and emerging ideas about the objectives of ESP teaching. In Part III, chapter 11 brings together the ideas examined in the preceding chapters and demonstrates how they can be used together to analyse and compare ESP teaching projects. In the chapters, content is organized around three themes: *Concepts, Research,* and *Applications.*

From chapter 3 on, each chapter includes a section entitled "Questions for Discussion and Projects" or "Questions for Discussion." These sections have been included to encourage readers to research and analyse the practices of ESP around them and to consider the ideas they draw on in their own teaching. References are given at the end of the chapters for readers wishing to read more on the topics covered and to provide additional resources to help with the questions for discussion and projects.

ACKNOWLEDGMENTS

I would like to thank series editor Eli Hinkel for her care and guidance in the preparation of this book. Her advice and suggestions have contributed enormously to the outcome of the work and any merits it may have. I wish to thank Naomi Silverman and the members of her editorial team at Lawrence Erlbaum Associates for their patience and help in the preparation of this book for publication. My gratitude goes to Rod Ellis, who encouraged me to write a book on ESP and for feedback in the initial stages. Finally, I would like to acknowledge all my colleagues in the Department of Applied Language Studies and Linguistics at the University of Auckland for their generous support.

This page intentionally left blank

I

PRELIMINARIES

This page intentionally left blank

Chapter 1

Introduction

This chapter argues that a book surveying ideas and options in ESP is a useful addition to the existing literature. To this end, a case is made that there are certain gaps in the ESP literature at present that the work aims to address and that it is timely to survey the range of ideas and options in ESP given the calls now being made for ESP to adopt a critical approach. The chapter also sets out the sources that influenced the present work.

AIMS AND AUDIENCE

This book has two aims. First, it aims to offer an examination of ideas influencing recent and present practice in ESP teaching and research. Second, it aims to illustrate the range of options that exist in ESP at present.

Teachers have at their disposal a range of options in designing ESP courses and materials. For example, two options in ESP in evidence today are genre-based approaches to course design and deep-end classroom methodology.

Genre-based approaches focus learners' attention on text types, or genres, that occur in target discourse communities, that is, the work- or study-related groups the learners aim to enter or make progress in as a result of gains in their English language proficiency. In an academic discourse community, significant genres are typically term papers, small-scale research projects, seminars, and research reports. Members of discourse communities regularly communicate with one another and with the outside world. By doing so, they have developed specific communicative practices and mechanisms, that is, distinctive forms of discourse. It is understood that learners of English should try to emulate the ways of communicating of those who are already members of those communities, and thus ESP instruction focuses learners' attention on the genres used in target discourse communities, as these are seen to represent the typical forms of communication in them. ESP teachers lead learners in the analysis of sample texts to identify conventional formats and the collective mind-set for communication of the members of the communities they aspire to. Research and teaching based on analysis of genres in academic communities are described in Swales (1990) and on analysis of genres in professional settings in Bhatia (1993).

Some classroom methodologies make extensive use of simulations, such as case studies from law or business. Students are asked to perform the simulation from the outset with either no or minimal input from the teacher. This is termed deep-end strategy (Dudley-Evans & St. John, 1998, p. 190). Learners are cast into a situation where they need to use English in order to perform, a situation in which they have to communicate using whatever English they have at their disposal. In this way, teachers and learners can find out in what ways the learners' knowledge of English is sufficient for the task and in what ways it fails them. Instruction can then focus on the aspects of language that were problematic for the learners.

Each of these two options incorporates different ideas about language learning. The aim of this book is to present the various options seen in ESP at present (such as genre-based approaches and deep-end methodology) and to examine the ideas distinguishing them. This examination of theoretical ideas and the links between them and practice and research will be of particular use to students on teacher education programs. It will also be of interest to the growing numbers of teachers working in the field of ESP to serve as a basis for situating their own practices and approaches and surveying the field in which they work.

IMPETUSES

Why a book on ideas and options in ESP? There are two main impetuses behind this work. One comes from the gap in the literature on ESP. The field of EAP is surveyed in Jordan (1997) and of ESP in Dudley-Evans & St. John (1998). The surveys cover a wide range of topics but do not deal with theory and ideas in detail. The literature has tended to focus primarily on practical issues, a point noted by Dudley-Evans & St. John (1998): 'It is interesting and significant that so much of the writing has concentrated on the procedures of ESP and on relating course design to learners' specific needs rather than on theoretical matters' (p. 1).

Where there has been discussion of ideas in the literature, this discussion has mostly focused on which descriptions of language can best inform ESP. Different approaches to language description in ESP have emerged over the years. One early approach was based on counting the frequency of linguistic forms in a given register. Barber (1962/1985) identified the frequency of a number of syntactic forms in written scientific prose by analysis of a corpus of texts from a mixture of scientific disciplines (electronics, biochemistry, and astronomy) and genres. The approach was later critiqued for failing to identify the purposes for which the forms were used. Subsequent analyses (for example, Tarone, Dwyer, Gillette, & Icke's 1981 study of passives in astrophysics) aimed to identify both linguistic forms and the purposes for which they were used (Flowerdew & Peacock, 2001b). The history of ESP's adoption of such approaches has been a recurrent focus of interest in the literature. It is reported in Robinson (1991), Dudley-Evans and St. John (1998), and Flowerdew and Peacock (2001b).

Discussion of ideas of *learning* languages for specific purposes has been limited. Although reports of methodologies have been featured in the literature, connections between them and underlying views of learning have rarely been made (although a notable exception is Hutchinson & Waters, 1987). Swales' seminal work, *Episodes in ESP* (1985), reflects the preoccupations of ESP with practical aspects of course and materials design and with language descriptions. Approximately half the articles in this work address each of these two areas. One article in this work, 'Box Kites,' contains an interesting proposal for course and materials design—an example of a task-based project for engineering students at Kuwait University. Although the views of learning implicit in project work and task-based learning are worth exploring, there is little discussion of them.

Generally, ESP has not been much concerned with the debates and issues emerging in recent years in the field of second language acquisition (Dudley-Evans & St. John, 1998; Bloor, 1998). Published reports of research focusing on language acquisition in ESP have been limited. One exception is the study of interlanguage use in relation to discourse domains by Selinker and Douglas (1985). It has also been noted that few studies have set out to investigate the effectiveness of ESP courses (Dudley-Evans & St. John, 1998).

There is also limited discussion in the literature about the objectives of ESP teaching. In the early years of ESP, the objective was seen in terms of imparting linguistic knowledge with ESP functioning to reveal the facts about the linguistic features of subject-specific language (Swales, 1985). Later it was seen in terms of training students in communicative repertoires characteristic of target situations (Munby, 1978). More recently, proposals include the notion that ESP should teach students concepts from their discipline, as well as language, in order to develop their 'underlying competence' (Hutchinson & Waters, 1985). Beyond this, however, exploration of the objectives of ESP teaching has been limited. This book aims to work toward addressing these gaps. It sets out to examine ideas about learning and teaching as well as ideas about language in ESP.

A second impetus for this work comes from the attempts in ESP to reconcile its work with the critical orientation emerging in applied linguistics at present. Critical Applied Linguistics has as its goal analysis of the ways people are unfairly positioned socially, culturally, economically, and politically (Pennycook, 1997a). A number of writers have articulated concerns about the role of ESP in society. Ideological worries are surfacing and calls are being made for critical ESP. Master (1998) argues that inasmuch as English dominates today's world and is the established lingua franca of science, technology, and business, ESP 'holds a pivotal position in regard to the use or abuse of this power' (p. 716). In relation to the experience of teaching English for academic and scientific purposes in developing countries, Swales (1998) comments:

> I have belatedly come to recognize a certain self deception. . . . I believed working overseas in scientific English, as researcher, materials writer, and teacher, was, in essence, a culturally and politically neutral enterprise. In doing so, I conveniently overlooked the links between teaching technical languages and the manufacture and export of technical equipment. (p. 5)

Typically, ESP has functioned to help language learners cope with the features of language or to develop the competencies needed to function in a discipline, profession, or workplace. But does this mean that ESP has been a force for accommodation and that by helping learners fit into target discourse communities it has served the interests of the members of those communities? Has it served the interests of linguistically privileged in-groups? Benesch (1996, 2001) calls for a critical approach to EAP teaching and shows how teachers can lead learners to question and challenge the status quo. Given the growing concern about the social and political implications of ESP teaching and the emergence of critical approaches in recent years, it is timely to stand back from current practices in ESP teaching and to consider the ideas and theories behind them.

INFLUENCES

The approach used to examine ESP in this book has been influenced by two main sources. First, this book owes a considerable debt to previous work in the area of analysis of ideas and options in language teaching by Stern (1983, 1989, 1992). Stern proposes a framework for analysis of language teaching comprising three lines of inquiry: the idea of language, of language learning, and the function of language teaching. Following Stern, this book sets out to examine the following in ESP practice and research:

1. Ideas about language and the types of language descriptions drawn on.

2. Ideas about language learning and how they can be related to the literature on second language acquisition.
3. Ideas about teaching methodologies and objectives.

The work is also influenced by a social theory, *Structuration Theory* (Giddens, 1984). This theory is based on the idea that social groups are constituted and continually reproduced through recurrent practices. These practices are mutually understood and generally exist as taken-for-granted forms of behaviour. Although the understanding of these practices is most often tacit, knowledge about these practices can be reported also (Blaikie, 1995). In this theory, the goal of the social enquiry is to establish the mutual knowledge of the community, and the means to establishing this is through analysis of their recurrent practices. The world of ESP can be seen as a social group. It is constituted and reproduced through a number of conventionalised and recurring practices visible in course designs and classroom materials, as well as an established body of knowledge and literature reported as teaching and research projects in journal articles and in books. The task of this book is to analyse and illuminate the 'mutual knowledge' of this society—that is, to reveal the practices of the world of ESP teaching through examination of academic writing and research as well as ESP course designs and methodologies.

A detailed discussion of the elements contributing to the formulation of the approach used in this book can be found in chapter 2. The framework used to examine ESP in the book is presented in chapter 2, also.

This page intentionally left blank

Approach

Whereas General English Language teaching tends to set out from point A toward an often pretty indeterminate destination, setting sail through largely uncharted waters, ESP aims to speed learners through to a known destination. The emphasis in ESP on going from A to B in the most time- and energy-efficient manner can lead to the view that ESP is an essentially practical endeavor. Nevertheless, within ESP there are proposals and counterproposals, arguments and counterarguments about the nature of the destination (views of what is meant by knowing a language for special purposes) and the best way of getting there (views of learning and teaching). Thus, although practical in orientation, ESP, like any other language teaching enterprise, is based on ideas about the nature of language, learning, and teaching. The task of this chapter is to set forth the approach to examination of these ideas used in this book.

This chapter introduces three key elements of the approach used to examine ESP in this book. These are: (a) the (mainly) data-driven nature of the enquiry; (b) the reference to a social theory—Structuration Theory (Giddens, 1984), which, it is argued, offers a useful perspective for ESP; and (c) the framework by which ideas in ESP are examined and the work organized.

DATA-DRIVEN

The approach taken in this book is essentially data-driven. This is because ESP practice has marched ahead of discussion of ideas. It is, however, time to stand back from practice and make explicit the thinking behind it. Beaugrande (1997) draws attention to the fact that in many domains of human activity, practices are established before explanations are provided. A data-driven approach is inductive and aims to provide explanations of already occurring events. This book sets out to examine the practice of ESP. The aim is to examine examples of ESP courses, materials, and research projects and discuss the ideas of language, learning, or teaching they encapsulate.

STRUCTURATION THEORY

In recent years, the approach to language description for English for Academic Purposes developed by Swales (1990) has been embraced by ESP. This approach has an evolving theory of language use in discourse communities, such as specific academic or professional groups, and views language as genres characterized by communicative purpose and distinct patterns of moves in them. The key linguistic unit in this approach is *genre*—a type of communicative event, identifiable by its communicative purposes and recognized as such by the members of the discourse community that use it. Through the targeting of genres in specific discourse communities, ESP has tried to provide valid language description for learners. Originally, the focus of genre-based approaches to ESP was tied to the analysis of text types. More recently, ESP has adopted a more dynamic view of genres, seeing them as "subject to change and adaptation, by the participants, in contrast to the somewhat static original text-bound conceptualization" (Flowerdew & Peacock, 2001b, p. 16). There has been increasing research interest in ethnographic approaches to the description of genres. This entails moving beyond purely language-based description to description of the context of use as well. This focus on how genres emerge and develop demands a vision not just of language and texts but also of society and how it functions. In short, it needs to be related to a social theory.

One major social theory informing the genre approach of Swales is *Structuration Theory* (Giddens, 1984). This is a theory of action and, like a number of other such social theories, addresses the question of how it is that "all competent members of society are able to act, interact, and understand the meaning of what they do" (Cohen, 1996, p. 211). Theories of action can be differentiated into two subcategories: those that argue the significance of subjective consciousness in action, and those that argue the importance of social conduct (praxis). The former assert the primacy of mental acts in directing action. The latter assert that social processes rather than mental acts are most influential; and the human mind does not have unrestricted powers to direct human action (Cohen, 1996). Giddens' structuration account of the constitution of society is an example of the latter.

Structuration theory addresses the subject of enduring practices in social life and argues that the things that happen or exist in social life are produced through enacted forms of conduct. According to Giddens (1984), societies (society at large as well as subsocieties within it such as ethnicities, genders, and, in our case, academic, professional, and workplace communities) are constituted and continually reproduced through recurring and largely taken-for-granted forms of behaviour such as genres. These forms of behaviour or social practices emerge, develop, and eventually die away over time in relation to the needs of the members of the society as they deal with the practical aspects of their day-to-day existence. This social theory is rooted in the interpretive paradigm and based on abductive approach (Blaikie, 1995). Social life is construed as a routine and a skilled performance. This is described by Blaikie (1995):

> Social life is a skilled performance which is made possible because competent members of society are practical social theorists who modify their theories about practical aspects of daily life on the basis of their experiences. The mutual knowledge which social actors use to negotiate their encounters with others and make sense of social activity is regarded as the fundamental matter of social science. The social scientist cannot begin to describe any social activity without knowing what social actors know, either what they report or tacitly assume, while engaging in the social activity. (p. 188)

Members of societies need to know the 'rules of the game' — they need to know how to produce acceptable forms of communication and action.

> A player in a game knows a particular rule for the game, when he knows how to play according to that rule, when he knows how to go on . . . to know the rule is to know then what one is supposed to do in all situations to which that rule applies. . . . A person may grasp a rule through observing regularity in what people do. (Giddens, 1979, p. 133)

According to Giddens (1984), members of a society have two types of knowledge. They have *practical consciousness,* tacit understanding of conventionalized procedures. They also have *discursive consciousness.* They can put into words these skills and procedures they have mastered and construct their own theories from their experiences. However, it is only during critical periods when routines break down that this kind of consciousness surfaces (Cohen, 1996). The analyst aims to establish the mutual knowledge of the society. This is done by illuminating practical consciousness and inferring the conventionalized procedures rather than listening to the members' views as to what the procedures are and taking this as fact (Blaikie, 1995).

Structuration theory is used here in two ways. Firstly, the theory can be used to explain a genre-based approach to teaching ESP. ESP is concerned with preparing students to enter target discourse communities (academic, professional, and workplace) with distinct and evolving communicative practices. Our ESP students can be seen as would-be participants in discourse communities. To participate, they need to become skilled performers. Genres and discourse generally are taken-for-granted forms of conduct by which the target academic, professional, and workplace communities are constituted. ESP learners, in order to participate in the societies they aspire to, need to know the rules of the game regarding these genres. To become skilled performers, they must be introduced to the rules of the game and thus the task of ESP can be seen as researching and teaching these rules. If ESP teachers and researchers can provide valid descriptions of skilled performance and ESP learners can acquire the elements of this performance, they can join the subculture and become part of the production of that society. Structuration theory and the concept of genres as taken-for-granted forms of behavior that are constituted and reproduced by a discourse community are discussed in some detail in chapter 5.

Second, structuration theory offers a useful perspective for the analysis of options and ideas in ESP in this book. The world of ESP can be construed as an established community, with its own evolving and taken-for-granted forms of conduct that are constituted in recurrent teaching practices, methodologies, and research interests. This book attempts to explicate the ideas behind these forms of conduct and shed light on the practical consciousness of the ESP teaching community.

FRAMEWORK FOR ANALYSIS

The framework used in the present work to examine ESP is heavily influenced by two frameworks developed for examining general English language teaching, those of Stern (1983, 1992) and Richards and Rodgers (1986).

Stern (1983, 1992) proposed a general conceptual framework for language teaching that comprised four key concepts: language, learning, teaching, and context. These were argued to be the basic building blocks of language teaching. Stern recognized that these concepts are often implicit in acts of teaching or in policy decisions practice, rather than explicitly stated. Stern argued that in order to compare and contrast different teaching practices, the concepts of language, learning, teaching, and society that underpinned those practices needed to be identified.

Stern argued that language teaching requires, first, a concept of the nature of language. How language is treated in the curriculum varies according to the fundamental beliefs held. For example, it may be treated analytically or synthetically. Language may be treated mainly as a set of grammatical constructions or discourse structures or sounds. Sociolinguistic aspects of language use, such as appropriateness, may or may not be attended to. Language teaching involves, second, a view of the learner and the nature of language learning. Third, it involves a view of language teaching specifying the role given to the teacher and a description of teaching. Last, it involves a view of the context of teaching.

Ideas	Types of description	Options
Language		
	Systems	Types of linguistic organization, such as sentence level grammar and patterns in text
	Uses	Units of language use, such as speech acts and genres
Learning		
	Conditions	Settings needed for language acquisition, such as linguistic or social environments
	Processes	Mental or social procedures used in language acquisition
Teaching		
	Methodologies	Types of teaching strategies
	Objectives of teaching	Roles played by ESP teaching

FIG. 2.1.   Framework for analysis of ideas and options in ESP.

Richards and Rodgers (1986) discuss approaches in language teaching. They identify the two main components of an approach: (a) a theory of the nature of language (an account of the nature of language proficiency and an account of the basic units of language structure), and (b) a theory of the nature of language learning (an account of the psycholinguistic and cognitive processes involved in language learning and an account of the conditions that allow for the successful use of these processes).

The remainder of this section sets out the *Framework for Analysing ESP* used to examine ideas and options in this work. The framework is intended to serve a number of purposes:

• To provide the categories with which different ESP teaching operations can be interpreted in fairly general terms.

• To help ESP teachers define their own ideas and perspectives on ESP teaching, and locate their own version of ESP.

• To enable ESP teachers and other professionals in the field to identify their position in regard to the various issues and options in the field, for example, where they position their own work in terms of the type of language description or view of the processes of learning in ESP it is based on.

• To enable ESP teachers to analyze and interpret documentary evidence of ESP, such as policy statements, education department initiatives, school mission statements, textbooks, methodological prescriptions, and curriculum statements.

Figure 2.1 shows that this work is organized into three areas: ideas about language, learning, and teaching ESP. In each area two different types of descriptions or explanations are given.

Chapter 3

Issues in ESP Course Design

This chapter examines issues related to four topics in ESP course design. It examines first the topic of language varieties, that is, descriptions of language use in specific academic, workplace, or professional environments. Second, it examines the topic of needs analysis, the type of investigation ESP curriculum developers use to identify the gap between what learners already know and what they need to know in order to study or work in their specific target environments. Curriculum developers use findings from needs analyses to help them specify the content of syllabuses. Third, it examines the topic of the syllabus. A number of different types of syllabus have been identified in the literature. Finally, it examines the topic of wide- versus narrow-angled course designs. Narrow-angled courses are devised for learners with very similar needs and are highly specialized. Wide-angled ESP courses are devised for learners with needs that are only somewhat similar and less specialized. The chapter concludes with discussion of specific and specifiable aspects of ESP.

VARIETIES OF LANGUAGE

The term *variety* refers to registers of language use, such as English in banking, English in medicine, English in academic settings, and everyday conversation. According to Bloor and Bloor (1986), there are two perspectives on the term *language for specific purposes.* One is that a specific-purpose language is based on and extends from a basic core of general language (the common core plus). The second is that all language exists as one variety or another and that there is no basic core ('general-purpose') language.

The Common Core Plus

It can be argued that there is a common core of general language that is drawn on in all areas of life and work. This can also be referred to as 'basic' language. Figure 3.1 shows a representation of common core language and its relationship to language varieties (Pitt Corder, 1993).

The inner section represents basic language and includes common words and sentence structures that can be used in all situations. The common core is represented as a general pool of language of high frequency items that predominates all uses of languages. Pitt Corder (1993) described this view as an abstraction. He argued:

> The utility of such a notion is rather doubtful. If, for example, a learner wishes to converse with lawyers in a foreign language, then those items which are part of legal language are central to his needs; many of them, however, have very low 'relative frequency' in 'the language as a whole.' (p. 66–67)

The idea that different varieties of English are based on a common set of grammatical and other linguistic characteristics has been widespread (Bloor & Bloor, 1986). The idea is reflected in the following quotation from Quirk, Greenbaum, Leech, and Svartik (1972), who argued that learners need to come to grips with basic English before they study English for specific purposes:

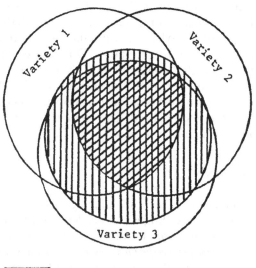

▨▨▨▨ 'Common core' of the language

▥▥▥▥ Learner's required repertoire

FIG. 3.1.   Common core view. From *Introduction to Applied Linguistics* (p. 66) by S. Pit Corder, 1993, Harmondsworth: Penguin. Copyright © 1973 by S. Pit Corder. Reprinted with permission.

Attempts to teach a 'restricted' language ('English for Engineers') too often ignore the danger in so doing of trying to climb a ladder which is sinking in the mud; it is no use trying to approach a point on the upper rungs if there is no foundation. (p. 29)

Coxhead and Nation (2001) categorize vocabulary for teaching and learning into four groups of words: high frequency words, academic vocabulary, technical vocabulary, and low frequency vocabulary. They argue: 'When learners have mastered control of the 2,000 words of general usefulness in English, it is wise to direct vocabulary learning to more specialized areas depending on the aims of the learners' (pp. 252–253).

All Language is Specific Purpose

A second perspective is that there is no common core of language preexisting to varieties. The core is, rather, an essential part of any one of the innumerable varieties of the language (Bloor & Bloor, 1986). In short, 'basic' language is what is present in all varieties of English, where the varieties overlap. All languages are learned in some context or another. There is thus no 'basic' variety-less English, there is no 'general English' or English for no specific purposes. All English exists as some variety or another. Bloor and Bloor (1986) assert:

All language learning is acquired from one variety or another, even if it is 'classroom English' variety. A language learner is as likely to acquire 'the language' from one variety as from another, but the use of language, being geared to situation and participants, is learned in appropriate contexts. This view supports a theory of language use as the basis of language acquisition theory. (p. 28)

According to Bloor and Bloor (1986), teaching a specific variety of English (ESP) can start at any level including beginners. Moreover, learning from the specific variety of English (for example, English for doctors, English for hospitality), is highly effective as learners acquire structures in relation to the range of meanings in which they are used in their academic, workplace, or professional environments. Figure 3.2 represents this second perspective. The figure shows three varieties of English (V1, V2, and V3).

NEEDS ANALYSIS

ESP is understood to be about preparing learners to use English within academic, professional, or workplace environments, and a key feature of ESP course design is that the syllabus is based on an analysis of the needs

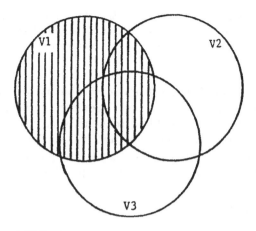

|||||||| Learner's required repertoire

FIG. 3.2. Language varieties view. From *Languages for Specific Purposes* (p. 20), by M. Bloor and T. Bloor, 1986. Reprinted by permission of Trinity College, Dublin, Ireland.

of the students. Thus, in ESP, language is learnt not for its own sake or for the sake of gaining a general education but to smooth the path to entry or greater linguistic efficiency in these environments. As the syllabus is based on needs, it is likely to be motivating for learners, who see the obvious relevance of what they are studying. Moreover, most ESP courses are subject to time constraints and time must be effectively utilized (West, 1994). As students in ESP classes often have restricted time to learn English, it makes sense to teach them only the bits of English they need. Thus the task of the ESP course developer is to identify the needs of the learner and design a course around them.

A number of needs analysis studies are reported in the ESP literature. Chia, Johnson, Chia, and Olive (1999) report their investigation of the English language needs of medical students in Taiwan. Sakr (2001) reports a study into the English language needs of textile and clothing industry workers in Cairo, and Evangelou (1994) reports a project to explore the English language needs of nurses.

Needs analysis studies have investigated the perceptions of language needs of different parties and have often revealed differing perceptions. Ferris (1998) investigated the differing perceptions of students and faculty of students' academic aural/oral needs for university study in number of colleges in the United States. Basturkmen (1998a) investigated student and faculty perceptions of the English language needs of students in the Faculty of Engineering and Petroleum at Kuwait University. Jasso-Aguilar (1999) investigated the perspectives of maids and the institutional representatives of the hotel in Waikiki in which the maids worked.

Li So-mui and Mead (2000) report the needs analysis they conducted to help them prepare an ESP course for students of textile and clothing merchandising in Hong Kong. Their project set out to obtain information on the types of communication required in the industry. They used a range of research methods to collect data including questionnaire surveys, telephone interviews, analysis of authentic correspondence, and visits to the workplaces of the merchandisers. The study revealed that the merchandisers used written English far more than spoken English in their work; that fax and telephone calls were more common channels of communication than e-mails and letters, and that there was a high use of abbreviations in written communication.

Some needs analyses follow ethnographic principles and aim for a 'thick description' of the target environments (Johns & Dudley-Evans, 1991). This approach to needs analysis involves in-depth ethnographic data collection methods such as observations and exploratory interviews. Examples of this type of needs analysis are Jasso-Aguilar's study (1999) of the language needs of maids in a hotel in Waikiki, Ibrahim's study (1993) of language needs in the manufacturing industry in Japan, and Kurtoglu's study (1992) of seminar speaking needs in a Turkish university.

Needs analysis in ESP has been critiqued and a number of issues identified in this seemingly neutral enterprise. Some of the criticisms and issues are:

- The information too often comes from the institutions themselves, who already have definite expectations about what the students should be able to do, and thus needs analysis serves the interests of the institutions, often at the expense of the learners (Auerbach, 1995).

- Language training for specific purposes can be a covert means to channel immigrants into marginal occupations, ensuring that they only have sufficient English to perform specific low-wage jobs and do not have good enough English to be able to move out of these jobs (Tollefson, 1991).

- The learners are often asked for their perceptions of needs but they may not be reliable sources of information about their own needs, especially if they are relatively unfamiliar with the job they are to perform or subject they are to study (Long, 1996).

- Objective needs are not necessarily the same as subjective needs or wants. For example, engineering students may objectively need to deal with written texts concerned with technical matter but may want to read topics in English on other general interest subjects. Using technical texts, topics, or tasks may turn out to be demotivating.

- Language needs are not learning needs. Although learners will need to use certain language structures or features in their target environments, this does not mean that they are ready to acquire them (Hutchinson & Waters, 1987).

- Asking learners about their language needs can be problematic because they may lack awareness or metalanguage to describe these needs in any meaningful way. It is improbable that students with unsophisticated knowledge about language would make sound decisions about their needs (Chambers, 1980).

- Language use in specific situations is simply too unpredictable to be identified in any certain terms. ESP has sometimes produced a rigid view of language needs and failed to take account of the variation of language use that exists in any target situation. A striking example of a rigid approach to analysis of language needs is seen in Munby's Communicative Needs Processor (1978). This approach involved the attempt to identify not only the English language functions that would be needed (for example, by a waiter working in a Spanish tourist resort) but also the actual linguistic formula for realising these functions.

- Perspectives of needs vary and the needs analyst has to decide whose perspectives to take into account in designing ESP courses or synthesize divergent perspectives (Jasso-Aguilar, 1999).

- Basing course designs on needs analysis may lead to language training rather than language education. Learners are trained to perform a restricted repertoire of the language rather than develop underlying linguistic competence of the language because they are deprived of the generative basis of language (Widdowson, 1983).

- Needs analysis is a means of fitting outsiders into the communicative practices of linguistically privileged in-groups. Needs analysis purports to be a neutral enterprise but in fact is often used by institutions to get others to conform to established communicative practices (Benesch, 2001).

- Needs analyses are not theoretically neutral. It can be argued that "any system of needs analysis is related to the theory of the nature of language" (West, 1994, p. 2). One needs analyst may aim to identify the language functions used in a particular environment whereas another may aim to identify high frequency syntactic features or lexical items occurring in the same environment.

TYPES OF SYLLABUSES

One of the fundamental questions for language teaching is what language is to be taught. In order to specify what language will be taught, items are

---

1. consists of a comprehensive list of

   - content items (words, structures, topics)

   - process items (tasks, methods)

2. Is ordered (easier, more essential items first)

3. Has explicit objectives (usually expressed in the introduction)

4. Is a public document

5. May indicate a time schedule

6. May indicate preferred methodology or approach

7. May recommend materials

FIG. 3.3.   Characteristics of a syllabus (from *A Course in Language Teaching*, by P. Ur, © 1996, Cambridge University Press, p. 177).

typically listed and referred to as the syllabus. Figure 3.3 shows a fairly standard view of the syllabus. Graves (1996) discusses the language curriculum and syllabus. She describes the curriculum as a broad statement of the philosophy, purposes, design, and implementation of the entire language teaching program and the syllabus as a specification and ordering of content of a course.

The seemingly straightforward procedure of specifying and ordering content involves, however, embracing one or more of a number of theoretical stances. In this respect, syllabus is aligned to the overall 'philosophy' of the course or courses. The 'items' or units teachers and course developers specify as course content and how they organize them reveal their ideas of the nature of language and learning. If they construe language as a set of communicative purposes, they would probably list various pragmatic functions (speech acts) of language (such as request, report, and describe) as course content.

Syllabuses can be synthetic (language is segmented into discrete linguistic items for presentation one at a time) or analytic (language is presented whole chunks at a time without linguistic control; Long & Crookes, 1992). Designers of analytic syllabuses believe the language content for a course should not be prespecified because language cannot be atomized into discrete particles for 'learning.' Rather, language should be approached holistically and teaching should proceed from the whole to the parts (Freeman & Freeman, 1989). Those who embrace the view that learning occurs when learners acquire individual items of language one by one and later combine them might opt for a synthetic syllabus that lists the linguistic items to be learnt. Those who embrace a view that learning occurs when learners perceive patterns in language samples and induce rules from them might opt for an analytic syllabus and list items that do refer not to language units but to some other sort of unit, such as task, situation, or topic.

When teachers and course designers opt for a synthetic approach and list items for the syllabus, the type of items listed reveals their ideas about what is important in two ways:

1. The types of items listed reveals ideas about the basic units of language and understanding of what 'packages' language naturally comes in. Is language best seen as the expression of intended actions of individual users (speech acts) or as patterns of language use that emerge in group practices over time (genres)? Does language come in sentences or texts?

2. The selection of items included reveals ideas about what is important. We may list pragmatic functions indicating a view of language as the intended actions of individual users (speech acts). However, as the number of possible pragmatic functions is very long, we need to select the pragmatic functions we see as the most important. We may feel that knowing how to request factual information and responding to requests to it are essential elements and thus include them in our list. This might indicate our orientation to an idea that language for specific purposes is concerned first and foremost with conveying factual information—the referential function of language. We may think that offering condolences or eliciting sympathy are somehow less essential and not include them, indicating a view that language for specific purposes is not about social purposes.

The academic, workplace and professional environment to which ESP students are headed may be little different from other environments in regard to the importance of social intercourse. It has been taken for granted that ESP teaching should focus on 'hard' language functions rather than 'soft' social functions. Halliday (1973) uses the terms the *referential* and *instrumental* functions of language. The first refers to language used to convey facts and knowledge; the second refers to language used to get things done. It has been assumed that social functions are less important than referential or instrumental functions in teaching ESP. However, recent applied linguistic research investigated the social functions language is used for in workplace environments and showed their importance (Holmes, 1999). Holmes (1998) reports on a study of the function of humor in the workplace. A study by Linde (1988) found that pilots' use of mitigation (politeness formula to soften the force of utterances) correlated to safety levels. The more mitigation the pilots used, the higher their safety performance records became. A study of spoken interaction in a factory setting (Pascal Brown, 2001) revealed that half of all talk was social. The spoken interaction of the factory manager illustrates this. Fifty per cent of the exchanges the manager participated in were social. Social exchanges were an important means by which the manager got the work in the factory done.

As it is not possible to teach all of a language, teachers and course designers must be selective. Nowhere is this more so than in ESP teaching, with its emphasis on specific purposes and the limited duration of most ESP courses. It is often by selecting what to teach that language teachers show their notions of what language is and their beliefs as to what is important in language learning. This point was also made by Hutchinson and Waters (1987), who claimed that specifying course content was value laden and revealed our notions of what language is and how language is learned. In short, the selection of course content reflects our ideas of language learning. See Fig. 3.4.

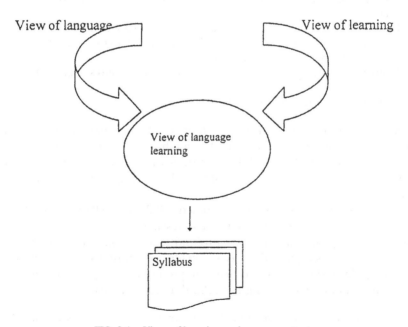

FIG. 3.4. Views of learning and course content.

Based on their observations of general English language courses, Brown (1995) and Richards (1990) list the following types of syllabuses. They also point out that courses are often based on a combination.

Structural (organized primarily around grammar and sentence patterns).
Functional (organized around communicative functions, such as identifying, reporting, correcting, describing).
Notional (organized around conceptual categories, such as duration, quantity, location).
Topical (organized around themes or topics, such as health, food, clothing).
Situational (organized around speech settings and the transactions associated with them, such as shopping, at the bank, at the supermarket).
Skills (organized around microskills, such as listening for gist, listening for specific information, listening for inferences).
Task- or activity-based (organized around activities, such as drawing maps, following directions, following instructions).

In EAP teaching, Flowerdew and Peacock (2001a) list the following types of syllabus:

Lexico-grammatical (organized around structures and vocabulary).
Functional-notional (organized around language functions and notions).
Discourse-based (organized around aspects of text cohesion and coherence).
Learning-centered (organized on what the learners have to do in order to learn language items and skills, not the items and skills themselves).
Skills-based (organized around particular skills).
Genre-based (organized around conventions and procedures in genres) as units of analysis).
Content-based (organized around themes).

Some syllabus types (structural, functional, notional, discourse- and genre-based) list the language to be taught. However, this is only one possible way to go. White (1988) identifies three options, listing content (forms, situations, function, and topics), skills (language or learning), or methods.

One methods option is the task-based syllabus, a syllabus type that is widely embraced at present. The task-based syllabus comprises a list of tasks (for example, giving instructions or following directions) that the students will perform. It is argued that tasks provide a purpose for using language meaningfully and that through struggling to use language to complete the task, the students acquire language. Prahbu (1987) explains:

Task-based teaching operates with the concept that, while the conscious mind is working out some of the meaning content, a subconscious part of the mind perceives, abstracts, or acquires (or recreates, as a cognitive structure) some of the linguistic structuring embodied in those entities, as a step in the development of an internal system of rules. (pp. 69–70)

Long and Crookes (1992) argue that task-based syllabuses in ESP specify 'real world tasks.' By contrast, in general English language teaching, the precise definition of the tasks is not a primary concern. Whereas in general English language teaching tasks are chosen for the pedagogical value, in ESP they may be chosen for their relevance to real world events in the target environments.

NARROW- AND WIDE-ANGLE COURSE DESIGNS

A course developer is faced with a group of students who are planning to study English for Academic Purposes (EAP). The course developer can divide the students into classes according to their respective disciplines. She or he could make two English for Specific Academic Purposes (ESAP) courses, English for engineering studies and English for social science. The course developer might further divide the groups. The engineering students could be split into English for computer engineering, chemical engineering, and civil engineering classes. Or the course developer might not group the students according to discipline at all and prefer to design a English for General Academic Purposes (EGAP) program. Another course developer is faced with a group of mixed experienced medical professionals. Should the developer divide them into subdisciplines—nurses, doctors, and medical technicians—or simply split them up into proficiency levels and focus on general medical English rather than English for doctors, English for nursing, and English for medical technology? The question is how specific, or narrow angled, ESP courses should be.

Some approach the question of specificity as a practical problem related to the specificity of needs. Dudley-Evans and St. John (1998) state that where needs are limited, a narrow-angled course may be appropriate and the course can legitimately focus on a few target events and use content or topics from one discipline. Where the needs are more general, the course can focus on a wider range of target events and use content and topics from a range of disciplines.

Others approach the question by referring to research findings. Clapham (2001) reports on research investigating the effect of background knowledge on reading comprehension in EAP. The investigation revealed that although students generally achieved higher scores on texts from their subject areas, this was not always the case, and sometimes students did better on texts that were outside their subject area. Clapham concluded that as texts vary widely in terms of their specificity and students vary widely in terms of their background knowledge, English for General Academic Purposes (EGAP) may be preferable to English for Specific Academic Purposes (ESAP).

Ferris (2001) describes two approaches used in designing ESOL academic writing classes in the United States. The first focuses on developing a set of generalized academic writing skills with the expectation that the learners will transfer these general skills and strategies to writing tasks in their own specific discipline (EGAP). The second focuses on teaching students to analyze and imitate the norms of the specific discipline they wish to enter (ESAP). Ferris surveyed U.S. universities to find that although most writers of scholarly publications advocated the second position, in reality, the majority of academic writing programs followed the more generalized approach.

SPECIFIC AND SPECIFIABLE ELEMENTS IN ESP

Needs analysis in ESP often focuses on the skills learners need to study or work effectively in their target environments. Bosher and Smalkoski (2002) report a needs analysis to investigate the speaking and listening needs of immigrant nurses attending a nursing degree program in the United States. Some of the needs identified were:

- Using paralinguistic features of communication (stress and intonation, and volume and rate of speech) in a clinical setting, especially with elderly patients.
- making 'small talk' with clients.
- Understanding clients who speak nonstandard dialects of English.
- Understanding the instructors' directions and following through with step-by-step procedures in performing clinical tests. (p. 64)

Flowerdew and Peacock (2001a) report that skills-based approaches have been particularly important in EAP and point to the fact that many learners in South America have traditionally needed only a reading knowledge of English. Studies often focus on identifying the skills needed for a particular workplace or study in a discipline. See, for example, the metareview of research into lecture comprehension in EAP (Tauroza, 2001). Flowerdew and Peacock (2001a) identify a number of reading skills that research has shown to be important for EAP learners including:

- Using existing knowledge to help understand new information.
- Recognizing text structures.

- Skimming for gist.
- Scanning to locate specific pieces of information.
- Distinguishing more from less important information.
- Reading selectively according to the purpose for reading.
- Distinguishing facts from opinions.
- Distinguishing main ideas from evidence.

Jordan (1997) lists skills involved in academic listening, including the ability to identify:

- The purpose and scope of lectures.
- The topic of lectures and follow topic development.
- The relationships among units within discourse (major ideas, generalizations, hypotheses, supporting ideas, and examples).
- The role of discourse markers in signaling content of a lecture (conjunctions, adverbs, gambits, and routines).

But are skills 'specific purposes'? Arguably the academic reading and listening skills listed here are used in any number of reading and listening situations. For example, reading film reviews would involve the reader in distinguishing facts from opinions. In listening to a friend in everyday conversation telling a personal narrative story, the listener again needs to identify the purpose of the talk and identify the relationship among units. What differs between listening in general everyday situations and in academic lectures is not the nature of the microskills being utilized but rather the type of text involved (in this case, a lecture or a story).

In analyzing needs, ESP curriculum designers identify which microskills from a general pool of skills used across a range of environments are important for a particular group of ESP learners. However, if a course aims to develop language skills, instruction needs to offer more than practice opportunities. This argument was made by Field (1998) in relation to listening. Unless a course sets out intentionally to foster the development of skills, should it be termed a skills-based course? In my own teaching experience when working on a writing course for engineering students at Kuwait University, the expected outcomes for the course were writing products, such as abstracts and recommendation reports. The microskills involved in producing an abstract (for example, extracting relevant information in reading) were practiced extensively as students prepared their abstracts and recommendation reports, but teaching did not deliberately foster students' development of these skills.

What are the specific elements in English for Specific Purposes? Figure 3.5 shows elements I argue are specific or simply specifiable. ESP instruction

Language System	specifiable
Language Use	specific
Language Skills	specifiable
Content (conceptual and cultural)	specific

FIG. 3.5.   Specific and specifiable elements in the ESP curriculum.

is oriented to helping learners become more aware of language use and conceptual content (including cultural content) critical in the workplace, academic, and professional environments, and disciplines to which they are headed. For example, instruction for the nursing students reported in Bosher and Smalkoski (2002) was oriented to cultural content. One of the needs the English for nursing studies course sought to address was 'making small talk with clients.' What constitutes small talk in healthcare situations is a question of content. The nursing students need to know what topics are appropriate for nurse–patient interaction and in which circumstances small talk is seen as appropriate. In workplace, academic, or professional environments and disciplines, certain language forms and features may occur more frequently than others and certain skills are used more often than others. These can be identified but they are not exclusive to those environments or disciplines. They are specifiable elements.

SUMMARY

This chapter has highlighted some of the issues involved in ESP curriculum development. It can be argued that language varieties are based in and extend from a common core of language. Or it can be argued that language varieties are self-contained entities. Needs analysis can be seen as an entirely pragmatic and objective endeavour to help course developers identify course content that is truly relevant to the learners, or it can be argued to have a bias in favour of the institutions and may overemphasize objective needs at the cost of subjective needs. It can be argued that syllabuses should specify content (what is to be taught). Or it can be argued that they should specify method (how language is to be taught). Some argue that the ESP courses should be as narrow-angled as possible. Others argue that this is not practical or that it is unnecessary as learners can transfer what they learn from a more general course to their own highly specific area at a later stage.

QUESTIONS FOR DISCUSSION AND PROJECTS

1. Do you agree that learners generally should acquire words of general usefulness in English before they embark on learning vocabulary in specialized areas?
2. If you were conducting a needs analysis in preparation for developing an ESP course, what practical steps would you take to ensure that you gather the perspectives of all the different parties (such as the learners, institutions, and teachers)? What would you do if there were significant differences in the perspectives of the parties?
3. Review the course book that you are currently using in your ESP class. What type of syllabus is it based on? If it is organized around one element in particular (for example, skills or grammar), how are other elements integrated into the design?
4. Interview a teacher or course developer who has conducted a needs analysis for an ESP situation. Find out what type of needs the analysis aimed to identify and whose perspectives were investigated.
5. Do you think that ESP courses should incorporate a focus on the 'soft' social purposes or should only focus on 'hard' purposes, such as transmitting information?
6. Discuss with colleagues any problems you envisage in devising wide-angled ESP courses (for example, English for General Academic Purposes or English for General Healthcare Professionals) and whether you think you could overcome them.

FURTHER READING

- A general introduction to course design and different types of syllabuses is offered in chapter 10 in Hedge (2000).
- A review of practices in needs analysis is provided in West (1997).
- Coxhead (2000) reports on a study to identify general academic vocabulary. This study was based on a corpus of texts from academic journals and textbooks in a range of disciplines from arts, commerce, law, and science.
- Hyland (2002a) argues the case for greater specificity and narrow-angled ESP course designs. A discussion of the advantages and disadvantages of narrow- and wide-angled course design in ESP is given in Basturkmen (2003).
- A range of issues in LSP course design and testing are examined in Basturkmen and Elder (2004).

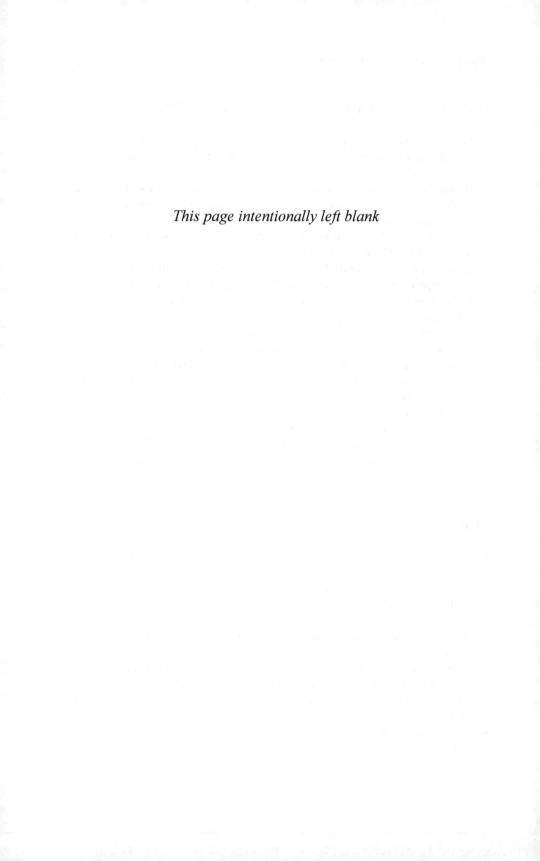

This page intentionally left blank

II

IDEAS AND OPTIONS

This page intentionally left blank

SECTION A

Language

This page intentionally left blank

Chapter 4

Language Systems

ESP teaching often takes, as a point of departure, the analysis and description of language systems. Hopper (1987) defines language systems as a set of abstract structures present for all speakers and hearers that is a prerequisite for the use of language. This chapter examines three language systems evident in ESP teaching and research. The first two of these, grammatical structures and core vocabulary, are examined together first, and the third, patterns of text organization, is examined in the last section.

GRAMMATICAL STRUCTURES AND CORE VOCABULARY

Concepts

Hedge (2000) points out that in general English teaching, there has been a revival of interest in grammar in recent years and yet for many teachers, grammar has always been a key focus of their instruction. It has been a traditional idea that second-language instruction should focus on a set of basic sentence-level grammatical structures (for example, verb tenses, conditional clauses, noun phrases) and core vocabulary. This idea has featured in ESP instruction also.

One early approach to ESP, Register Analysis, was concerned with identifying and teaching the grammatical structures and vocabulary seen as of central importance in scientific and technical writing. The approach was premised on the ideas that although scientific and technical writing has the same grammar as general English, particular grammatical structures and vocabulary items are used more frequently. Analyses of scientific and technical texts by Barber (1962/1985) showed that the passive tense is used more frequently in such writing than in general English and identified a set of subtechnical vocabulary items that were more likely to occur.

35

Research

An EAP-oriented research project aimed to assess whether first-year students from a range of disciplines in an Indonesian university had a sufficiently well-developed English vocabulary for academic study purposes (Nurweni & Read, 1998). The study investigated how well the students knew a set of core vocabulary items. It aimed to establish how many words the students knew and their depth of knowledge of the words, such as their understanding of the range of uses of the words. The study measured the students' knowledge of vocabulary items in the General Service List (West, 1953) and the University Word List (Xue & Nation, 1984). The former represents the 2,000 most frequent words in English and the latter comprises 800 subtechnical words commonly used in academic English. The researchers estimated that the 2,800 words from the combined lists constituted an essential reading vocabulary as these words cover around 92% of the words in academic type texts. To test the students' vocabulary size, words from the combined lists were given in sentences. The students were required to provide a translation in their first language of the target words. To test the students' depth of knowledge, students were presented with the targeted items plus a list of other words, some of which were semantically associated (similar in meaning) with the targeted items. The students were required to identify the associated words. In addition, students were asked to compose a sentence using targeted items. The results of the study showed that, on average, the students knew only 60% of the first 1,000 most frequent words in English, 37% of the second 1,000, and just 30% of the university words list. In general, they knew an average of 1,226 (44%) of the 2,800 words on the combined lists and could correctly identify fewer than two of the four word associates. They did not have a vocabulary size of 4,000–5,000, a level generally regarded as necessary for reading academic texts.

Applications

In language teaching instruction, a focus on grammatical structures is often seen in courses based on structural syllabuses in which particular grammatical structures are targeted and presented to the learners. For example, in the course book *Elementary Technical English* (Webber, 1983), one grammatical structure targeted for instruction is the present passive. The form is highlighted and presented with a number of examples concerned with engine mechanisms, for example, 'the piston is pushed down by the fuel and air' and 'the fuel and air are compressed by the cylinder' (p. 88). In the course book for learners of Business English illustrated in Fig. 4.1, learners are presented with a range of structures for making comparatives in English. The structures are highlighted and learners are required to

A 🔲 ⊙ Listen to someone from Transworld Freight Forwarders talking about different types of transport and complete the grid.

Transport	Advantage	Disadvantage
a	fast	expensive large quantities not possible
b	suitable for heavy goods or large quantities	.... ports expensive delays common
c	door-to-door service	....
d	economical use of labour	no door-to-door service

B Study these ways of comparing things.

Transporting goods by air is much faster than by sea.
Transporting goods by sea is not as fast as by air.
Transporting goods by air is the fastest method.

Transporting goods by air is more expensive than by sea.
Transporting goods by sea is not as expensive as by air.
Transporting goods by air is the most expensive method.

N.B. good – better – best; bad – worse – worst

Make some sentences comparing air and road transport. Use the words in the box to help you like this:

Transporting goods by air isn't as cheap as by road.

cheap   fast   difficult   dangerous   slow   expensive   easy   safe

Which method of transport is

a the most flexible?
b the most reliable?
c the most environmentally friendly?

Compare your answers with a partner.

C Match the type of cargo to the symbol.

Types of cargo

1 perishable goods ☐
2 hazardous goods ☐
3 livestock ☐
4 high value cargo ☐
5 fragile goods ☐
6 flammable goods ☐

Can you think of other examples of these types of cargo?

D You work for a consultancy firm. Write short reports on the best methods of transport for your clients.

1 Leuwan Florist of Holland deals in flowers and supplies the European market.
2 Johnson Chemicals of Britain distributes chemicals to the European market.
3 Heriot Meats of New Zealand supplies the Middle East and Japan with livestock and frozen meat.
4 ACR of Taiwan supplies the world market with computer monitors.

Don't forget to give reasons for and against the different means of transport.

FIG. 4.1.   Sample material: Forms of Transport (from *Further Ahead Learner's Book* by S. Jones-Macziola & G. White, © 1998, Cambridge University Press, pp. 34–35).

37

understand how the structures are formed and then to produce sentences of their own using these structures.

PATTERNS OF TEXT ORGANIZATION

Concepts

This section examines structures underlying written or spoken texts. A text can be defined as a stretch of language. Scollon and Scollon (1995) argue that language is inherently ambiguous. They distinguish between external and internal ambiguity. *External ambiguity* is related to the contexts in which meaning is to be interpreted. *Internal ambiguity* is related to the ways parts of a text relate to each other.

Early interest by linguists in how people interpreted and dealt with external ambiguity in texts led to the notions of schemata and scripts. These are described by Hoey (2001). A *schema* is the knowledge people have about certain types of event such as eating out at a restaurant. A *script* is the knowledge people have about how these events typically unfold. In the case of eating out at a restaurant, the sequence of events would include being seated, getting the menu, and giving an order. This knowledge is formed from people's experiences in life. When a person hears the word 'waiter,' this acts as a trigger to activate that person's knowledge of these events, which is then brought to bear in helping the person interpret a text (for example, when reading about someone's experience in a restaurant) or participating in discourse (for example, when having a dialogue with a waiter).

First example of a two-sentence text (contrived):

> *We had no record of the booking.*
> *We were offered a suite on the top floor for a reduced price.*

According to schema or script theories, a person would interpret the second sentence by recalling his or her preexisting knowledge of hotels and check-in difficulties and would use this knowledge to understand how the second part is related to the first. The person uses his or her real-world knowledge to deduce meaning.

Hoey (2001) argues that schema and script concepts are of limited practical value for the analysis of texts and teaching reading and writing. The number of scripts or schemata a person may need is potentially limitless. In practice, it is not possible to list and describe each and every one.

A second explanation of how people decode a text is that they deal with its internal ambiguity. It is argued that there exists a generic set of patterns of text organization. Various terms have been used in the literature to denote these patterns, such as *macro structures* (McCarthy & Carter, 1994), *clause relations* and *basic text structures* (Winter, 1994), and *culturally popular patterns* (Hoey, 2001). Those subscribing to this view of how people deal with the ambiguity in language would argue that people interpret the second part of the example text by recourse to their knowledge of pervasive patterns of organization in texts. In this case, they interpret the first part as a problem statement and this triggers recall of a problem–solution type of text organization. The second part is interpreted as the solution to the first part.

Patterns of text organization can be construed as a set of structures similar to (but longer than) sentence structures. Like descriptions of sentence-level grammar, descriptions of patterns of text organization highlight what are assumed to be core features of language. Hoey (2001, p. 6) describes this generic set of patterns as the 'nuts and bolts' of language, similar to the rules of syntax. Knowledge of the nuts and bolts can allow people to have a generalized set of expectations about text patterns. To interpret a text, the reader or listener follows the connections between the parts and relies on his or her knowledge of the ways that parts (clauses, sentences, or longer segments) are typically organized in text. One typical pattern of text organization is cause–result.

Second example of a two-sentence text (contrived)

> *Interest rates on mortgages have fallen to less than 8%. The number of house sales is expected to increase.*

In this example, the second sentence would probably be interpreted as a result of the event in the first sentence. This relationship could be overtly signaled with conjunctions, such as, *in consequence, thus, therefore.* Even without overt signaling, the reader can infer this relationship. Some patterns in English texts described by Winter (1994) are 'general–particular' (general statement followed by example) and 'preview–detail' (introduction to an idea followed by particulars). The note shown in Fig. 4.2 illustrates a preview–detail pattern.

According to Hoey (1994), the pattern 'situation–problem–solution–evaluation' is very common in English expository-type texts. Other pervasive patterns identified by Hoey (2001) are 'goal–achievement,' 'desire arousal–fulfillment,' and 'gap in knowledge-filling.' Texts reporting scientific experiments may illustrate the latter pattern. They describe, first, what was known about the phenomenon in question and what remained unknown. They describe, second, the test or experiment conducted to try to 'fill the gap' and the results obtained.

Research

Three research studies related to the idea that there exists a set of patterns of text organization are described next. The first two studies investigated

Dear Helen and Paul.

* The one thing we didn't have a price on last week was the glass splash-back behind the hob. ** The templated and installed price is $772 + GST, allowing for 2 cutouts for power points/switches.

You may have any color.

Regards

*preview ** detail

FIG. 4.2.   Note illustrating preview-detail pattern.

the use of patterns of text organization in the writing of learners of English. The third investigated the link between patterns of text organization and text comprehension.

Kobayshi (1984) reports on a study to investigate differences in U.S. and Japanese college students' use of general–specific patterns. The study involved four groups of students:

1. U.S. college students,
2. Japanese advanced ESL students in the United States,
3. English majors in Japan, and
4. non-English majors in Japan.

Groups 1 to 3 wrote in English and Group 4 wrote in Japanese. The groups' writing of the same narrative and expository essay tasks was examined for use of general–specific patterns. Results showed differences between the groups. Group 1 mostly used a general–specific pattern, Group 4 mostly used a specific–general pattern; Groups 2 and 3 used both of these patterns but Group 3 used the specific–general pattern more often. The results indicated that one source of lack of coherence in Japanese learners' written English is their preference for specific–general rather than general–specific text structures.

A study by Hirose (2003) examined the patterns of organization Japanese students used in writing argumentative essays in Japanese and English. The participants in the study were third- and fourth-year students majoring in British and American Studies in a public university in Japan. All the students had previously studied 1- or 2-year English academic writing courses that focused on organizing and developing essays. The participants wrote an argumentative essay, first in English and then at a later date in Japanese, on the same topic—whether high school students should wear school uniforms or not. A number of analyses were made of the essays. One analysis aimed to identify which of three patterns of organization the students used. These patterns were: Explanation (the writer's opinion followed by a supporting reason), Specification (the writer's opinion and a preview statement of a supporting reason followed by a supporting reason), and Induction (a supporting reason before the writer's opinion). The first two patterns were considered to be examples of a deductive writing style and the third pattern was seen as an inductive style. The results showed that, generally, the participants preferred the Explanation pattern when writing in both English and Japanese. However, whereas all the participants used the Explanation pattern when writing in English, 3 students used the Induction pattern when writing in Japanese. The use of the Specification pattern was not seen. Hirose suggests that the writing instruction had probably influenced the students' writing, and that as it is not difficult for Japanese students to learn to use deductive patterns, L2 writing instruction of this aspect of language can be effective.

Second-year students in an English for Science and Technology course in a school of engineering in Spain were the subject of a study by Martinez (2002). Martinez investigated whether the Spanish first language students' knowledge of text structure (macropatterns) and signals in English affected their comprehension of written text. The study made use of a written text about body-water loss in humans. The original text comprised 21 ideas units. Martinez reformulated it into five new texts, four of which displayed common patterns of text organization (cause–effect, chronological sequence, compare–contrast, and problem–solution) and signaling words (such as, as a result, second, in contrast to, a serious problem is). One text had neither a typical pattern of organization of ideas nor any signals of text organization. This text was simply a collection of idea units in a random order. The students read one of the texts and then were required to write everything they could remember about the information in the text in complete sentences showing how the ideas were related to each other. They were also asked if they had recognized the organization of the text they had read and, if so, to identify that organization. The results showed that the students who had received the text with a random organization of ideas were less able to recall the information contained in the text. The results also showed a

1. What is the current percentage of research papers published in English—as opposed to other languages?

30%   40%   50%   60%   70%   80%   90%

Now read on.

The Role of English in Research and Scholarship

[1]There are many claims that a clear majority of the world's research papers are now published in English. [2]For example, in 1983 Eugene Garfield, President of the Institute for Scientific Information (ISI)[1], claimed that 80% of the world's scientific papers are written in English (Garfield 1983). [3]Comparable estimates have recently been produced for engineering, medicine, and nonclinical psychology.

[4]It is not clear, however, whether such high percentages for English provide an accurate picture of languages chosen for publication by researchers around the world. [5]The major difficulty is bias in the databases from which these high percentages are typically derived. [6]The databases are those established by the major abstracting and indexing services, such as the ISI indexes and Medline, which are predominantly located in the United States. [7]As a result, these services have tended to pre-select papers that (a) are written in English and (b) originate in the northern hemisphere. [8]For these two reasons, it is probable that research in languages other than English is somewhat underrepresented.[2] [9]Indeed, Najjar (1988) showed that no Arabic language science journal was consistently covered by the Science Citation Index in the mid-1980s. [10]We can hypothesize from the previous discussion that the role of English in research may be considerably inflated. [11]In fact, several small-scale studies bear this out: Throgmartin (1980) produced English percentages in the 40% range for social sciences, and Velho and Krige (1984) showed a clear preference for publication in Portuguese among Brazilian agricultural researchers. [12]A complete bibliography on schistosomiasis, a tropical disease, by Warren and Newhill (1978) revealed an English language percentage of only 45%. [13]These studies would seem to indicate that a more accurate percentage for English would be around 50% rather than around 80%.

[14]However, so far no major international study exists to corroborate such a conclusion. [15]Until such a study is undertaken—perhaps by UNESCO—the true global picture of language use in research publication will remain open to doubt and disagreement. [16]Until such time, nonnative speakers of English will remain uncertain about how effective their publications are in their own languages.

2. The passage consists of four short paragraphs, which deal in turn with the four parts of the standard problem-solution text (see table 4). Are sentences 1, 4, 10, and 14 the key sentences in the passage? If not, which other sentences might you suggest? Would you suggest sentence 13, for example?

3. Where do you think the author (John) is more convinced? Is it in the statement of the problem in paragraph 2, or in the statement of the solution in paragraph 3? Why do you think this?

4. List (using name and year) the citations used by the author. Do you have any criticisms?

5. Do you have any evidence to contribute about the languages of publication in your own field? What about the languages of research publication in your home country?

TABLE 4. Parts of a Problem-Solution Text

Situation	Background information about claims for research English
Problem	Reasons for doubting the accuracy of the figures
Solution	Alternative data leading to more accurate figures
Evaluation	Assessment of the merits of the proposed answer

1. The Institute for Scientific Information (ISI) publishes the *Science Citation Index* (SCI), the *Social Science Citation Index* (SSCI), and the *Arts and Humanities Citation Index* (AHCI).

2. The ISI itself has concluded that it may underrepresent useful research from the lesser developing countries by a factor of two (Moravcsik 1985).

FIG. 4.3. Sample material from *Academic Writing for Graduate Students*, by J. M. Swales and C. B. Feak, 1994 (pp. 58–59). Copyright © University of Michigan Press. Reprinted by permission.

significant relationship between students' recognition of the type of text organization used and their ability to recall information from the text. Martinez concluded that the students' conscious knowledge of patterns of text organization led to positive effects on their reading performance.

Applications

Ideas about how people interpret texts can be related to top-down approaches to second-language reading instruction and listening comprehension. Top-down approaches encourage learners to make use of their background knowledge to help them understand a text. Richards (1990) compares top-down approaches to bottom-up approaches that view comprehension as a process of decoding successive levels of language from sounds to words and sentences to reach meaning. Hoey (2001) describes the reading comprehension process as follows:

> As readers interact with a text they formulate hypotheses about how the text will develop, and these hypotheses help them understand and interpret the text as they continue reading. . . . Learners need therefore to be encouraged to develop the appropriate hypothesis-forming skills and not to treat reading as an exercise in language practice only. (p. 31)

From a top-down perspective, background knowledge can take a number of forms, including knowledge of the topic of the discourse, the situation, and the script (Richards, 1990). It can also include knowledge of patterns of text organization. Martinez (2001) argues for an approach to teaching reading in ESP based on raising students' awareness of macropatterns in text.

Postexperience ESP students (those who already have experience in their target workplace, professional, or academic discipline) can be encouraged to exploit the preexisting schemata and scripts they have formed when reading texts in their specialist subjects. Preexperienced ESP students have no such ready scripts to which to refer. Teachers of such students may wish to introduce them to generic patterns of text organization to help them deal with the ambiguities that arise in interpreting texts.

Figure 4.3 illustrates second-language writing instruction that focuses on patterns of text organization. The material is taken from a course book on academic writing for postgraduate students (Swales & Feak, 1994). The material highlights the pattern situation–problem–solution–evaluation, which is referred to as the 'standard' pattern. Instruction centres on a sample text to illustrate this pattern (Item 1). The form of this pattern is highlighted in Table 4 (in Fig. 4.3). In Item 2 students are asked to consider whether the paragraphs' initial sentences are key sentences in signalling the macropattern.

SUMMARY

This chapter examined ESP teaching and research focused on three language systems. In teaching, primary concerns are to describe and ensure learners are familiar with what is perceived to be the generative base (or core) of English. In research, a primary concern is to identify and describe the core structures. One of the major advantages of this approach to language description at a practical level is that fairly heterogeneous groups of ESP learners can be taught together; for example, English for General Academic Purposes courses can be offered rather than English for Specific Academic Purposes courses. This is because a set of basic structures, words, or generic patterns of text organization is seen as the core, and knowledge of them is a prerequisite to language use regardless of specific domain. In line with this argument, study of language use in the specific domain can come later.

QUESTIONS FOR DISCUSSION AND PROJECTS

1. What role does the teaching of grammatical structures play in the ESP classes you have taught? How were particular structures for instruction targeted and was grammar instruction integrated with other elements?
2. Do you agree that academic vocabulary is largely acquired through reading and study? What role can and should classroom-based instruction play? Should size of academic vocabulary be used as a criterion in giving or limiting access to a course of academic study for second-language learners?
3. Select an authentic text you might use with a particular group of ESP learners to develop reading skills. Analyse the text for occurrence of generic patterns of text organization, such as situation–problem–solution–evaluation and signals of text organization. Discuss how you could use your analysis to develop activities for the reading class.
4. Examine samples of your own writing of expository text (descriptive type writing) in English to identify whether you use general–specific or specific–general patterns of text organization. Form a discussion group, preferably with teachers from different first-language backgrounds, and compare your findings. What might be the implications of culturally variable differences in text organisation for writing instruction in the ESP classroom?
5. Instruction focused on language systems is, by definition, concerned with general features of language. Although such instruction may occur in the ESP classroom, it should not really be considered as ESP. Discuss.

FURTHER READING

- Swales (2001) traces the history of linguistic research in EAP. A good introduction to written text analysis can be found in chapter 6 of Mc-Carthy (1991).
- Hoey (2001) describes patterns of text organisation that transcend individual genres and text types.
- Chapter 5 of Swales' (1990) book discusses the concept of schemata in relation to genres and acquisition.
- Connor (2002) examines developments in the field of contrastive rhetoric, which includes a review of studies investigating patterns of text organization across cultures.

This page intentionally left blank

Language Uses

This chapter concerns descriptions of language use and functional explanations of language. Descriptions of language use focus on the communicative purposes people wish to achieve and how people use language to achieve them. Brown and Levinson (1988) describe functional explanations as attempts to locate sources outside the linguistic system that determine how language is organized. ESP has embraced such ideas. Bloor and Bloor (1986) write:

> One thing that ESP, in conjunction with a great deal of recent research into the language of special fields and genres, has shown is that the most important factor for the effective use of the language is that the learner has command of the ways in which the grammar of the language works to perform specific functions in specific contexts. (pp. 21–22)

A functional view of language is seen in different types of linguistic enquiry in ESP, descriptions of speech acts, genres, and social interaction formulas used in professional, workplace, or academic environments. It is also seen in attempts made to identify how words are used in particular disciplines (such as economics or law) to express discipline-specific concepts. This chapter describes the different types of descriptions and examines ESP-oriented research and teaching linked to them.

SPEECH ACTS

Concepts

ESP instruction and research often includes a focus on identification of the speech acts (also termed *functions*) used in target environments and the language exponents preferred by members of those environments to realise them. For example, a study by Blue and Harun (2002) set out to

47

identify common patterns and regularities found in language for hospitality purposes. By examining the interactions between hotel staff and customers at hotel receptions, the researchers identified speech acts frequently occurring in this environment (such as check-in and check-out functions, requests for information, and dealing with complaints and criticisms) and features of the language used to express them.

Speech act descriptions are concerned with the communicative intentions of individual speakers or writers and are defined by the purposes for which the speaker uses the language, for example, to make a request, to apologize, and to report. Speech acts are a key concept in the field of pragmatics, the study of speaker intent and what speakers mean when they use a particular linguistic in context (Hatch, 1992). Pragmatic meaning can be contrasted to semantic meaning. Semantic meaning is the sum of the lexical and syntactic meaning that an utterance has in isolation (Stenstrom, 1994). This is an utterance's 'fixed context-free meaning' (Cook, 1989, p. 29). The utterance "It's really late" can be understood at two levels. At a semantic level, it expresses the proposition that time passed and it is late at night. At a pragmatic level used by a guest at a dinner party, it may function to excuse the guest or to refuse an offer of food or drink.

Generally, the person responsible for first generating interest in pragmatic meaning was the philosopher Austin (Thomas, 1995). Austin's ideas about language are presented in the book of lecture notes entitled *How to Do Things With Words* (1962). Austin was interested in the fact that people do not use language just to state things but to do things, in other words, to perform actions. He also noted that people manage to communicate effectively. He argued that we should try to understand how people communicate effectively with the linguistic resources available to them (Thomas, 1995). Austin (1962) observed that an utterance simultaneously involves three elements: (a) locutionary (the actual words uttered), (b) illocutionary (the force or intention underlying the utterance), and (c) perlocutionary (the effect of the utterance on the listener). In a hectic workplace situation, someone may say 'I'm busy' (the locution), meaning 'you're disturbing me' (illocutionary force). The visitor disappears and gives apologies for the interruption (perlocutionary effect).

Although speech acts may directly address the listener, in reality many are indirect. Indirectness occurs when the meaning that is expressed and the meaning that is implied do not match (Thomas, 1995). To illustrate, a speaker, on hearing a knock on the office door, may want the visitor to go away, but in many situations it would be thought too abrupt or rude to say so directly. Therefore alternative, indirect means are used. These means often stress the ability or desirability of having an action performed or the speaker's reasons for having the action performed. In the earlier example, the speaker uses an indirect speech act and says, 'I'm busy' (the speaker's reasons for having the hearer leave) rather than use a direct means, such as, 'You're disturbing me.'

Hatch (1992) explains that following Austin, Searle (1969) classified utterances into a small set of functions. The set included directives (attempts by the speaker to get the hearer to do something, for example, requesting, asking, and insisting), commissives (commitments by the speaker to do something, for example, promising, offering, and threatening), representatives (commitments by the speaker to the truth of something, for example, reporting, denying, and believing), declaratives (acts that bring about a new state of affairs, for example, 'I hereby declare you man and wife' and 'I resign'), and expressives (acts indicating the speaker's attitude to something, for example, liking, welcoming, and apologizing).

The terms *pragmalinguistics* and *sociopragmatics* were coined by Leech (1983). Kasper and Rose (2001) define these terms from a language teaching perspective. The term pragmalinguistics refers to the linguistic resources needed by a speaker to express illocutions. The resources include lexical, syntactic, and prosodic means of softening or strengthening the force of an utterance and means of expressing it formally and informally. The term sociopragmatics refers to the speaker's ability to use and interpret speech acts appropriately according to social norms. This ability is described by Kasper and Rose (2001) as 'the social perceptions underlying participants' interpretation and performance of communicative action' (p. 2). It includes a speaker's assessment of social factors such as status and degree of imposition of the speech act. Thus, knowing how linguistically to form a polite request is pragmalinguistic, whereas knowing when, to whom, and what it is polite to request is sociopragmatic.

Research

One thrust of speech-act-based research in ESP has focused on identification of speech acts that occur in a target situation. For example, Sullivan and Girginer (2002) investigated the language used by pilots and air traffic controllers. Examination of authentic recordings of transactions between pilots and air traffic controllers at a nearby airport revealed that requests occurred frequently. Information about what kinds of requests were used and how language was used in them was then used to inform the development of instructional materials for the ESP course that Sullivan and Girginer were developing for pilots and air traffic controllers.

In Applied Linguistics generally, a notable thrust of research interest in recent years concerns the acquisition of speech acts by second-language learners. The book *Pragmatics in Language Teaching* devoted to this topic appeared in 2001 and brought together articles on various aspects of the acquisition of pragmatics, such as the effects of different types of instructions in teaching compliments and compliment responses (Rose & Kasper, 2001).

There is a considerable body of research showing that non-native speakers differ from native speakers in their use of speech acts. Bardovi-Harlig (2001) reviews research (including research in an EAP setting) to identify four areas of difference. First, non-native speakers can differ in choice of speech acts. Investigation of students' use of speech acts in authentic academic advising sessions in university settings showed that native speakers used more suggestions than non-native speakers and non-native speakers used more rejecting acts. The research shows that native and non-native speakers can differ in the choice of semantic formulas they use when making speech acts. Bardovi-Harlig (2001) reports that research into academic advising sessions revealed that native speakers ranked the use of alternatives as the second most preferred strategy to reject suggestions made by an advisor. The use of alternatives was ranked fourth by non-native speakers, who ranked avoidance as their second most preferred strategy.

Crandall (1999) also investigated the use of speech acts by native and non-native speakers in academic settings. Crandall's study recorded and examined students' requests in meetings with university faculty. The study aimed to find out how students made requests and the difficulties non-native speaker students experienced in this. Crandall recorded naturally occurring talk between students and faculty when they met in one-on-one conversations during office hours. A number of requests were made during these office hours, including requests for extensions for assignments and to change the topics of projects. Part of the study had a sociopragmatic focus as it included investigation of whether the native and non-native speaker students approached the faculty directly or indirectly when making their requests. Findings revealed some differences. For example, only one of the non-native speakers used direct requests, compared to seven of the eleven native speakers recorded. The non-native speakers used more hints than native speakers to make similar requests, such as to ask for help with an assignment. One non-native speaker requesting a grade change hints, 'You see the mark is very low' (p. 121).

Applications

Ideas about speech acts underpin functional syllabuses. Two broad types of speech acts (functions) addressed in these syllabuses are acts typically but not exclusively found in speaking (for example, making suggestions and complimenting) and acts typically but not exclusively found in written language use (for example, defining and classifying).

Part of the rationale for speech-act-based and pragmatics-based teaching derives from observations by language teachers of the lack of correlations between students' knowledge of language systems and ability to communicate with others. Research has shown that despite high levels of grammatical competence, non-native speakers may still have difficulties in communicating because of a lack of ability to express speech acts appropriately (Bardovi-Harlig, 1990; Thomas, 1983). This may occur because they inappropriately transfer speech act realisations or strategies from their first language or have misconceptions about the target language (Crandall & Basturkmen, 2004). Whether and in what ways speech-act-focused instruction leads to learning is discussed in the metareview of the classroom research on second-language pragmatics instruction in Kasper (2001).

It has been noted that some speech-act-based courses and materials target pragmalinguistics with the aim of equipping learners with the linguistic resources to make a number of speech acts and to do so more or less politely and directly, but neglect sociopragmatic aspects (Crandall, 1999). For example, a study of the treatment of compliment speech acts in language teaching materials (Huang, 2000) found that although a number of course books offered descriptions of complimenting in English, almost none targeted sociopragmatic aspects of complimenting (gender and status differences in complimenting behaviours and appropriate topics for complimenting), despite the fact that there exists a considerable body of research findings on these aspects. Often, presentations of speech acts in language-teaching materials are based on an assumption of sociopragmatic universality (Boxer, 1995; Crandall, 1999; Riggenbach, 1990).

The teaching material shown in Fig. 5.1 comes from a course book targeting Business English Skills. In this material, a set of speech acts (functions) have been isolated for treatment. These include expressing opinions, asking for clarification, and making proposals. These acts, or functions, are presented as titles for the boxes. The task for the students is to place the 20 linguistic realizations (forms) into the appropriate boxes. Students will see that each speech act can be realized by a number of forms. This emphasizes the centrality of function, that is, intended action in language rather than forms. Students then are required to produce a diagram of a role-play around the speech acts. Following this, the students devise a role play of a speech-act event involving these acts. The material focuses the learners' attention on pragmalinguistic elements (the language that can be used to form the acts) but not sociopragmatic elements (social norms of use).

GENRES

Concepts

Dudley-Evans (1994) traces the origin of the term *genre* in ESP to a study by Tarone et al. (1981) that investigated the use of active and passive forms in journal articles in astrophysics. The study found that the communicative

Negotiating

Negotiating involves a number of language functions such as making proposals, inviting concessions and asking for clarification. Make a copy of the grid on page 55 and place the following sentences in the boxes (two sentences per box).

1 *I'm sorry, I didn't catch what you said.*
2 *I suggest that* we fix the price at 870 deutchmarks per dozen.
3 *I have no doubt that* our customers will appreciate this product.
4 *I can't go along with you/that.*
5 *If I were you I would* take note of what your competitors are doing.
6 *In return, we would hope that you* extend the warranty to 3 years.
7 *We were given to understand that* labour charges were covered by the warranty.
8 *That wouldn't be acceptable, I'm afraid.*
9 *That seems reasonable,* I suppose.
10 *What do you say we* work on the basis of a 90 day payment period?
11 *I'm afraid I'm not quite with you.*
12 *Have you thought of* the advantages of leasing?
13 *I'd like some more details about* your system of discounts.
14 *I think we could go along with that.*
15 *I really feel that* the packaging is too bright.
16 *If we did accept, we would expect you to* reciprocate by doubling the size of your order.
17 *Could you tell me some more about* your after-sales service?
18 *In other words,* I'm unable to improve upon my last offer.
19 *I'm rather surprised to see that* transport costs are not included in the price.
20 *What I mean is* that I'm not empowered to make that kind of decision.

FIG. 5.1. Sample material from *Executive Skills* (pp. 54–56), by P. Minkoff, 1994, Hemel Hempstead: Prentice Hall. Copyright © 1994 by Prentice Hall International (UK) Ltd. Reprinted by permission of Pearson Education Ltd.

purposes of the writers regulated the ways language was used in the texts. The scholar generally accepted as being responsible for developing a genre-based approach to research and pedagogy in ESP is Swales, whose book *Genre Analysis: English in Academic and Research Settings* (1990) has been seminal in the field.

A genre is understood to be a class of language use and communication that occurs in particular communities (Allison, 1999). The community in which a genre arises provides a label for it (Swales, 1990). So, for example, the medical community has a genre labeled 'case history' and the teaching

Making proposals and counter-proposals	Reformulating information
Expressing opinions	Inviting a concession
Disagreeing	Asking for clarification
Querying	Asking for further information
Offering advice	Agreeing

FIG. 5.1 *(continued)*

community has the 'end-of-year report.' The communicative purpose of a genre is seen as its defining feature, the feature that sets it apart from other genres, and that explains its form and features of language use (Dudley-Evans, 1994). Whereas speech acts were seen as deriving from the internal drives of the individual to achieve his or her communicative purposes, genres are seen as collective and socially derived.

Genre theory seeks to explain the texts used by groups or communities by reference to the functions of those groups or communities and their outlook on the world. For example, typical functions of academic communities include dissemination of research findings, provision of descriptions, and explanations of phenomena. These functions lead to certain forms of communication including the conference presentation and the research report.

Whereas speech-act categories are understood to be universal, as people in any language or language subgroup would want to make requests, offer advice, and so forth, the functions and outlooks of groups and communities are highly specific. Scollon and Scollon (1995) argue that groups (such as dealers in foreign exchange, the ESL teaching community, and U.S. corporations) develop their own idiosyncratic ways of communicating. Members develop set ideas about what constitutes acceptable and nonacceptable communication and reject communication and participants that do not fit in as confused or illogical. As time passes, the conventional forms of a genre attain the status of taken-for-granted facts.

A seminal article by Miller (1984), "Genre as Social Action," contributed to a reconsideration of the term *genre*. Whereas genre analysis had been concerned with categorizing text types in relation to how they are formatted or according to surface level textual features, genre analysis widened to become concerned with explanation of genre features in relation to the social context and led to a view of genres as typified responses to recurring situations constructed by members of a community (Adam & Artemeva, 2002). Approaches to genre analysis are now seen as existing on a continuum between, one the one hand, studies that are grounded in the analysis of texts and, one the other hand, those grounded in analysis of the context and the community in which the genre appears. The New Rhetoric Movement, which emerged from the 1980s mainly in English departments in U.S. universities, represents the contextual end of the continuum and has been influenced by social constructive theories that view scientific facts as socially and rhetorically constructed (Swales, 2001). Hyland (2002b) describes a social constructivist view of language as follows:

> Language is not just a means of self expression. . . . It is how we construct and sustain reality, and we do this as members of communities, using the language of those communities. The features of a text are therefore influenced by the community for which it was written and so best understood, and taught, through the specific genres of communities. (p. 41)

One social constructivist theory, *Structuration Theory* (Giddens, 1984; see chapter 2), argues that institutions have recurring practices (including those enacted by language, such as genres) and that each time those in the community participate in these practices, they become increasingly familiar with the cognitive perspectives of the community. Institutions are thus structured (produced, reproduced, and modified) as individuals participate in recurring practices.

To participate in the recurring practices of a community, individuals draw on the rules of play for those practices. The rules may be tacit, as in the form of habitual or socialized routines, or may be codified into 'standards.' Yates and Orlikowski (1997) discuss the relationship between members of community (termed *organizational members*) and genre rules:

> When organizational members write business letters or engage in meetings, they implicitly or explicitly draw on the genre rules of the business letter or meeting to generate the substance and form of their documents or interactions. They also, in effect, reinforce and sustain the legitimacy of those rules through their action. (pp. 390–391)

It is understood that genres not only result from the contexts in which they occur, but also they help constitute and shape those contexts. Thus there is interplay between context and genre (Freedman, 1999).

Genres are also understood to evolve and change in response to changes in the needs of the community (Dudley-Evans, 1994). A genre-based perspective on language does not mean that genres are seen as fixed and static. Genre rules constrain the communicative choices including choice of lexis, syntax, and content but they are not binding. Individuals can and do challenge and change these rules gradually. Thus there is potential for genre modification. Over time, because of that potential, new genres emerge and old ones die away (Miller, 1994).

Berkenkotter and Huckin (1993) present a set of principles for genre based on a synthesis of a number of diverse theoretical orientations (including Gidden's Structuration Theory). The principles are:

> Dynamism. Genres are dynamic rhetorical forms that are developed in response to recurrent situations in a community. They serve to give the community coherence and meaning. Genres change over time in response to needs.

> Situatedness. Our knowledge of genres is derived from and embedded in our participation in the communicative activities of daily professional life. As such, genre knowledge is a form of situated cognition that continues to develop as we participate in the activities of the ambient culture.

> Form and content. Genre knowledge embraces both form and content, including a sense of what content is appropriate to a particular situation at a particular point in time.

> Duality of structure. As we draw on genre rules to engage in professional activities, we constitute social structures (in professional, institutional, and organizational contexts) and simultaneously reproduce these structures.

Community ownership. Genre conventions are signals of a discourse community's norms, epistemology, ideology and social ontology. (p. 4)

Research

In recent years, much teaching and research in ESP has focused on the study of the genres used in academic groups and workplace or professional communities. Genres are seen as consistent forms of communication and the established practices of those in the groups and communities to which ESP learners aspire. Instruction in the genres used in the target communities is seen as a way ESP can help learners gain acceptance into those communities. Genre-based studies are concerned to identify structures and patterns underlying specific genres, that is, types of texts with distinctive communicative purposes, such as narratives, service encounters, research article introductions, and sales letters, and their role in the groups and communities that create and use them. Analysis is made of naturally occurring, multiple samples of the genre and by investigation of its communicative purposes and the expectations held for it in the community or group from which it has emerged. Genre-based studies have been widely used in research in specific disciplines including research into experimental scientific articles (Bazerman, 1988), genres in the tax accounting profession (Devitt, 1991), and memos in business offices (Yates & Orlikowksi, 1997).

Research into genres in ESP may include some or all of these procedures:

• Identification of the genres used by a specific community. This may include discussions with insider members of the community to identify which genres are highly significant for the group, the communicative purposes of these genres, and expectations held for them.

• Development of a corpus of authentic samples of the genre to be studied.

• Analysis of the recurrent patterns constituting the structure of the genre.

Figure 5.2 shows an adaptation of Swales' (1990) analysis of research article introductions. The right-hand column shows the moves and steps that Swales found typically occurred in this genre. The moves are actions taken to achieve communicative purposes. Collectively, the moves achieve the overall communicative purpose of the genre. The steps are the options that different writers use to make the moves. Swales' analysis revealed that research article introductions comprise a three-move pattern. Swales termed this pattern 'Create a Research Space' (CARS). The left-hand column shows procedures used in Swales' approach. The text is categorized

Categorize the text according to its overall communicative purpose	Example Research Article Introduction
Label the stages (moves) with functional labels	Move 1: Establishing the research field Move 2: Establishing a niche Move 3: Occupying the niche
Indicate any moves that are optional rather than obligatory	
Identify the steps an individual writer/speaker may make to realize any move.	For example Move 1: Establishing the research field By Step 1 claiming centrality of the topic and/or Step 2 making topic generalizations and/or Step 3 reviewing items of previous research

FIG. 5.2. System of analysis of research article introductions (based on Swales, 1990).

and the moves and steps are identified and labeled. In some cases, this is followed by investigation of the use of grammatical structures, vocabulary, and discourse in individual moves and steps.

Zhu (1997) investigated the sales letter genre in the business community in Mainland China. Zhu examined a corpus of 20 authentic sales letters in order to identify the sequence of moves in them and to offer an analysis of how the moves are structured. Using the approach to analysis developed by Swales (1990), Zhu identified moves in the letters according to their communicative purposes. The moves identified were:

1. Introductory section (optional)
2. Establishing credentials
3. Introducing the offer
    a. Offering product or service
    b. Evaluating product
    c. Offering incentives
4. Soliciting response
    a. Request
    b. Using pressure tactics (p. 552)

Zhu then analyzed the development of ideas in each of these moves, finding that generally the writers preferred a main-to-subordinate rather than subordinate-to-main sequence of ideas in the moves. Zhu's analysis allowed her to demonstrate that the structural development of the Chinese sales letter genre is basically linear and thus to offer evidence against Kaplan's (1966) argument of a generic Oriental written style in which a central idea is developed in a circular fashion.

Zhu's methodology included the step of consulting with 100 managers of enterprises in China. The managers were asked to identify the most and least successful letters from the corpus. The managers identified letters that conformed well to Zhus' model as the most successful.

A further example of a genre-based study that involved working with inside members of the discourse community is provided by Hafner (1999). Hafner investigated the writing difficulties of non-native speaker students studying law. The study investigated how these students performed on examination answers to 'problem questions' in Commercial Law. In the study, Hafner asked four qualified lawyers to write their answers to the same examination questions. Hafner then compared the sequence of moves and language use in both sets of data.

Samraj (2002) investigated research article introductions from two related fields, Wildlife Behavior and Conservation Biology, using the CARS model of Swales (1990). Samraj found variation between the two disciplines in the structure of the introductions. The introductions from Wildlife Behavior generally contained the moves given in the CARS model. The CARS model worked less well for the introductions from articles in Conservation Biology. Samraj relates the differences to the orientations of the two related disciplines. Wildlife Behavior is a theoretical field. It is a discipline in its own right and it has an established history. Conservation Biology, on the other hand, is an applied field. It is interdisciplinary and a relatively new subject. As a result, the introductions from Conservation Biology display a greater promotional function than those from Wildlife Behavior and thus are not well represented by the CARS model.

Applications

At the core of genre-based ESP teaching has been a concern to identify the genres that students will use in the target situation and then help students to deconstruct them in order to understand how they are structured, how the structure relates to the objectives (or communicative purposes) of the target group, what content the genres contain, and the linguistic devices and language use typical in them. Thus in ESP, if our students are a group of medical researchers, we try to establish which genres are important for them in their work (such as articles reporting research, research proposals, and grant applications) and then highlight the structures and features that typify those genres.

In addition to showing how genres are structured as products, instruction can also focus on the ways of thinking of the communities in which the genre occurs. Paltridge (2000) argues that as genres reflect a community's way of doing things, learners need not only to learn the linguistic formula for constructing a genre, they also need to go beyond the text to an examination of the social and cultural context and reach an understanding of the community's purposes for the genre and the institutional values and expectations placed on it. Teaching can thus serve in the "demystification of the epistemological conventions of certain disciplines" (Dudley-Evans, 1994, p. 229).

Genres are specific to the communities in which they arise. Each academic discipline, each workplace group and professional community serves a different function in society and thus their purposes vary, with resulting impact on the genres that arise in them. A research proposal in mathematics is different from a research proposal in history. A case study report in business is different from one in social work. Research, such as that of Samraj (2002), can reveal just how different the practice of a genre in one discipline can be from that in another. Genre-based teaching is thus often best suited for classes of ESP students with very similar needs who are all targeting similar workplaces, or the same profession or academic discipline.

One central concern for teaching is how best to help the learners acquire genres. There is increasing recognition that the descriptions yielded by genre analysis should not be simply presented to learners as formulas or prescriptions in the ESP classroom. Santos (2002) argues that methodology for genre-based teaching should aim to clarify but not prescribe genre features. It should aim to identify patterns typical in genres but should not try to impose them on the learner.

The material shown in Fig. 5.3 focuses on the genre of proposals in business environments. The lesson aims to help raise the students' meta-awareness of how this genre is organized and language used in it. Each move (termed *main stage*) is identified in terms of its communicative purposes.

In one respect genre-based descriptions are similar to speech-act descriptions. Both focus on communicative purposes or intentions. However, genre-based descriptions focus on the overall communicative purpose, and a genre is defined and interpreted in relation to this purpose. The material in Fig. 5.3 shows that for the business proposal, the overall purpose is on persuading the client of the need for the product/system. Because of the need to persuade the client of the need for the product/system, one major

Persuasive Proposals

Levels
High intermediate +

Aims
Learn the organization
of a solicited business
proposal
Learn what makes a
proposal persuasive
Practice summary
writing

Class Time
1½ hours

Preparation Time
45 minutes

Resources
Business proposal with
a clear problem-solution-
evaluation pattern

Proposal writing is one of the most common types of written documentation in the business world. Most textbooks on business communication highlight the specific sections of the proposal, such as the implementation of the suggested proposal, budget, and personnel. In contrast, this activity sensitizes students to the overall macrostructure of the proposal, that is, the problem-solution-evaluation organizational pattern (see Hoey, 1983) and the way it is realized in various sections of the report (i.e., letter of transmittal, executive summary, introduction, and conclusion). Students become aware of the various linguistic devices used in the three main stages of a proposal and learn that a persuasive proposal identifies a problem or need, proposes a feasible solution, and specifies the benefits of the proposed solution.

Procedure

1. Make three copies of the business proposal. In the letter of transmittal, executive summary, introduction, and conclusion, blank out (a) all the problem (or need) statements in the first copy, (b) all instances of the proposed solution in the second copy, and (c) all evaluative comments (i.e., benefits and advantages of proposed solution) in the third copy. Leave intact the main body of the proposal detailing the implementation, personnel, budget, and other information.
2. Divide the students into three groups of the same size.
3. Give each group a different blanked-out copy of the proposal.
4. Ask each group to fill in the section (i.e., problem, solution, or evaluation of solution) that is missing from its copy of the proposal.
5. Have one member from each group form a new group of three, so that each group contains a student responsible for writing a different section of the problem-solution-evaluation pattern.
6. Ask the three students in each new group to (a) compare what they have written with the original sections of the proposal that the two other members have and (b) discuss the similarities and differences they find. During this discussion stage, circulate among all the groups and take notes on the students' vocabulary usage, their summarizing techniques, and the quality of their end product.
7. As feedback, discuss the three-part organizational pattern, review summarizing and paraphrasing techniques, and emphasize key or useful vocabulary.

FIG. 5.3.   Sample material: Persuasive proposals. From L. Flowerdew, 1998 (pp. 148–149). Reprinted by permission.

move is to state the present problem, a second is to proffer a solution to that problem (the product/system), and the third move is to proffer an evaluation of that product/system. The material leads the students in analysis of the overall purpose of the genre and identification of the main moves included in it.

SOCIAL INTERACTION

Concepts

Descriptions of social interaction are concerned with the strategies and linguistic devices users of a language draw on to create and maintain interpersonal relations. There has been limited concern with this type of language description in ESP.

Brown and Levinson (1988) present a theory of politeness. They argue that speakers and writers have at their disposal a number of interpersonal strategies that they use to enhance, or at least not jeopardize, their social standing and their relationships with others. There are two types of politeness, positive and negative politeness. Positive politeness is driven by the desire to make the listener (or reader) feel good about him or herself. A speaker may, for example, use strategies to make the listener feel included or may praise the listener. Negative politeness is driven by the desire to avoid infringing on the listener's (or reader's) territory and asking for too much. Brown and Levinson argue that positive and negative politeness strategies are universal but that specific groups or communities make use of the strategies in different ways.

One interpersonal strategy is hedging. Brown and Levinson (1988) categorize this as a negative politeness strategy. This commonly recognized strategy involves the use of devices by writers or speakers to indicate a limited belief or commitment to the ideas or information they provide. Lakoff (1973) coined the term *hedging*, describing hedges as words that make things more or less fuzzy. A writer or speaker makes the statement, 'The time may have come to act.' He or she uses 'may' rather than saying directly, 'The time has come to act.' This can be interpreted in two ways. One interpretation is that the word 'may' is simply being used to signal modality. The writer or speaker is signaling how probable he or she believes the statement to be. The second interpretation is that the word 'may' is being used to hedge the proposition that the time has come to act. The use of the hedge is based on social considerations. The speaker has face concerns about making a direct statement with which others may disagree. Or the speaker feels a need to assume a tentative stance in interaction with the addressee.

Research

A number of ESP-oriented studies have examined the social strategy of hedging. They have shown that it is, as Hyland (1996) argues, best understood in relation to the institutional and professional contexts in which it is used.

One study, Vassileva (2001), investigated the different use of hedging in Bulgarian and English academic writing to find that academic writing in Bulgarian contained fewer hedges and more 'boosters' (devices to increase the pragmatic force of statements) than academic writing in English. Vassileva concluded that English academic writers feel a need to show more deference to their academic community than Bulgarian academic writers do.

Bloor and Bloor (1993) investigated the ways economists modify their claims. They found that the use of hedging was related to the type of claim made in economics. They identified two distinct types of claims in economics texts: field-central and substantive claims. Field-central claims (those related to modeling and interpretation) tend to be hedged, whereas substantive claims (those concerned with results) tend to be presented as bold and factual findings.

Myers (1989) studied the use of hedging in scientific writing about research, to find that hedges reflected the appropriate attitude for offering a claim to the scientific community. Myers argues that as the making of a claim of knowledge threatens the academic scientific community, the writer alleviates such threats by using hedging.

A study of academic speaking in seminars (Basturkmen, 1998b) identified the use of hedging in specific functions in interaction. One finding was that speakers used hedges to mask their opinion giving as opinion seeking.

Applications

Descriptions of social interaction are based on a concept of language as socially motivated. They are concerned with how speakers and writers interact strategically with their interlocutors and readers. Different social groups may vary in how they use strategies, and ESP teaching can introduce these ways to students. The task of such ESP instruction is to offer a description of how universal phenomena such as politeness and hedging are accomplished in specific disciplines and work environments. The teacher of a class of English for medical doctors may, for example, want to describe when hedges are used in doctor–patient talk and how doctors hedge when giving bad news to patients. The teacher of an English for economics class may want to focus on why and when predictions are hedged in economics forecasts, and the teacher of an English for business class may want to focus on how politeness strategies are used in business negotiations.

The teaching material shown in Fig. 5.4 focuses on hedging (referred to as 'minimizing'), a universal strategy serving to make messages less clear. The material presents ways those in a business environment might hedge their messages and also how they emphasize their messages, that is, make the message more direct. The aim of the material is to raise learners' awareness of hedging and show how this strategy can be realized in Business English.

The material first introduces the concepts of minimizing and maximizing and attempts to get students to recognize occurrences of them. It then shows students linguistic realizations for minimizing and emphasizing in a business context.

WORDS USED FOR DISCIPLINE-SPECIFIC MEANINGS

Concepts

This type of description is concerned with word or structure choice, which words or structures are commonly chosen, and the meanings or uses they have in specific disciplines, professions, or workplace environments.

ESP courses have, in past years, targeted the words and structures important in a given field. In early years, register analysis studies set out to identify frequently occurring lexical items and grammatical structures in a particular field. The premise underlying the approach was that although language use in a field—for example, science—is not different from general English, certain lexical items and structures would predominate by appearing more frequently (Dudley-Evans & St. John, 1998). This approach has been referred to as *lexicostatistics* (Swales, 1985, p. 2) and an early example was Barber's (1962/1985) study of language use in science.

With the development of concordancing software, it has become possible for researchers and teachers to scan in field-specific texts (for example, textbooks or research articles from biology), to identify which structures and words occur and co-occur most frequently. By studying the concordances, it is possible to identify how these items are used in the target environments. Take a hypothetical example—the word 'supply.' A concordance of general English might show that the word 'supply' most commonly occurs as a verb. Examination of corpora of economics texts may reveal that 'supply' is rarely used as a verb in economics. To take another example, we may find that in

Language knowledge

DR LINDEN
'Or thirdly, and this is what I
support, we could put forward a.
alternative proposal.'

1 You are going to hear eight short extracts from different presentations.
   you listen, decide whether the language in each extract is being used to
   emphasize or minimize the message, and complete the table. The first o
   has been done for you. Check your answers in the key on page 64.

Emphasize	Minimize
☐	a
☐	☐
☐	☐
☐	☐

IT MAY COME AS A SLIGHT
SUPRISE TO HEAR THAT YOU'VE
BEEN PICKED TO TAKE PART IN THE
COMPANY'S DOWNSIZING PROJE(

REDUNDANCY

Language focus Emphasizing and minimizing

Emphasizing

Strong adverbs intensify adjectives:
We've had an extremely good year.

Adverbs can be total, very strong, or moderate.

TOTAL
absolutely (fantastic)
completely (awful)
entirely (depressing)

VERY STRONG
extremely (good)
very (bad)

MODERATE
fairly (safe)
reasonably (expensive)
quite (cheap)

Minimizing

Look at the way the following expressions of degree
and uncertainty modify, or minimize, the message:

It seems we will have to delay the delivery.
*The Chief Executive Officer appears to have left the
country.*

It's just a little bit further.
We're going to reduce our staff a bit.

Perhaps we should consider resigning.
There might be another way.

I tend to think we should stop now.
*To some extent, the company has failed to realize its
potential.*

Intonation is also very important in giving more or les:
emphasis to what we say.

FIG. 5.4. Sample material: Emphasizing and minimizing. From *Effective Presentations* (pp. 38–39), by J. Comfort, 1995, Oxford, UK: Oxford University
Press. Reproduced by permission.

2 Add an adverb to these sentences to emphasize the message. Compare your answers with the key on page 64.

a This has been a good year. ••
b We have had a difficult time. •
c We have seen a disastrous decline in our profits. •••
d It was easy to achieve our objectives. •
e The announcement was unexpected. •••
f I've got some bad news. ••

Key

moderate •
very strong ••
total •••

3 Complete these sentences with words that will minimize the message. Compare your answers with the key on page 64.

a We _____ see things differently. _____

your experience is _____ limited.

b _____, you're right. But _____ we

_____ consider the long-term view.

c There's _____ time. _____ we

_____ discuss this question now.

Presentation practice

1 Change the language in this text to communicate the message more persuasively. Compare your version with the key on page 64.

The trouble with business today is that people don't have time. Companies have reduced their workforces so that fewer people have to do the same amount of work. This means that managers don't see what is happening around them. They need their time to work through their regular tasks and have no time to take on new initiatives.

Time for reflection is important. Decisions taken now not only affect today's business, they can also have an influence on business in the long term. Strategy is the concern of senior management when it needs to be the concern of everybody in the company.

2 Prepare and give a short presentation on a subject you feel strongly about. Use language, body language, and intonation to communicate your message clearly and persuasively.

FIG. 5.4 (continued)

general usage the word 'present' is very often used as a transitive verb—for example, 'We presented the results'—and that this verb is rarely followed by the proposition 'with.' However, if we established a corpus of texts written or spoken by medical practitioners, we might find that 'present' is often followed by 'with'—for example, 'She presented with severe weight loss' and 'The patient presented with pain in the upper right molar.' From this we might conclude that 'present with' occurs regularly in medical texts and that it carries a specific meaning in this discipline. Doctors report this meaning as roughly synonymous with the phrase 'having symptoms.' Sager, Dungworth and McDonald (1980) explain:

> To the extent that the organisation and structuring of knowledge is reflected in linguistic communication the semantic approach is an important area of investigation. In particular, it is necessary to clarify whether there are any linguistic means of signalling special subject language items, and if so what these are. . . . If special subject knowledge can be represented as systems of content form, we have to examine to what extent they also have separate systems of expression forms and under what conditions they can share elements of expression form, e.g. is 'energy' the same word when used by a doctor or a physicist, or under what conditions can 'velocity' and 'speed' be said to be synonyms? (p. 8)

Research

A number of studies have been conducted in ESP to identify words or structures of particular importance in various disciplines. The study by Tarone et al. (1981) set out to identify the occurrence of the passive in research writing in astrophysics. Research by Lindemann and Mauranen (2001) investigated the use of the word 'just' in academic discourse. Ferguson (2001) studied the use of if-conditionals in medical discourse.

A study conducted by Kirkgoz (1999) set out to identify words of particular importance for students of economics in an English-medium university in Turkey. The study set out to identify (a) high frequency lexical items in the texts the students would encounter in their studies and (b) the meaning these items carried in the field of economics. The data for the study comprised a corpus of textbooks used by the students and journal articles related to economics. From this, 75 high frequency 'content words' (nongrammar words) were identified. Kirkgoz argues that the importance of these words for the ESP learner (the prospective student of economics) is that they 'bear the main information load in expressing concepts of the target discourse community' (p. 148). Following on from identification of these key words, the study then sought to identify the 'shared frame of reference' of these words. This involved finding the frequency of the significant collocates of the word (that is, the surrounding words the key words were typically used with). From these collocations, Kirkoz was able to establish the 'concepts' central to meaning in the economic community.

One high frequency item was the word 'cost.' This word was found to collocate with the words shown in Fig. 5.5. In the figure, an asterisk (*) represents the positioning of the word 'cost.' Words found four positions on either side are shown on the right and left of the asterisk. One important concept for the members of the economics community that Kirkgoz investigated was 'opportunity cost.' The item carries a specific meaning in economics.

5 and	7 the	17 its	30 opportunity	*	38 of	10 capital	6 is	5 and
7 to	9 of	17 its	25 average	*	39 curve	12 the	9 the	10 the
4 but	5 it	6 and	22 the	*	15 curves	8 of	6 is	5 capital
2 been	3 point	2 assign	2 firms	*	2 equals	3 upward	3 to	2 given

FIG. 5.5. The use of cost in economics textbooks and journal articles (from Kirkgoz, 1999).

Applications

This type of description (the words and structures carrying discipline-specific concepts) can be seen in ESP teaching. Figure 5.6 shows material taken from a course book on academic writing for tertiary level students. The material focuses on how the word 'criteria' is used in academic writing. A concordance of 'criteria' is presented. Students are required to study the concordance and identify how it is used by finding patterns in the surrounding words. Eventually the students are required to create their own piece of academic writing using 'criteria' and other words focused on in the unit ('identification' and 'analysis'). The three words focused on have been selected on the basis of frequency of occurrence in academic writing and the meanings they carry in it.

SUMMARY

This chapter examined different types of description of language use evident in ESP today. One was description of the intentions of individual speakers or writers (speech acts). Another was the analysis of conventionalised text types and formats in different discourse communities (genres). Another was the description of the ways speakers and writers circumnavigate the terrain of interpersonal communication (social interaction). The last description was of the words or structures used in a particular environment or field to express concepts specific to it. All these types of description focus on language from the outside in. That is, they are concerned with the regularities or repetitions that occur in language use. Figure 5.7 shows a summary of the different types of language description described.

QUESTIONS FOR DISCUSSION AND PROJECTS

1. What links can you make between the language descriptions examined in this chapter and your own ESP teaching?

1 Which of the following statements do you think are correct? Tick your answer in the box.

Criteria are standards by which something can be judged	correct ☐ incorrect ☐
Criteria are rules for testing something	correct ☐ incorrect ☐
A criterion is justified criticism	correct ☐ incorrect ☐
A criterion is a necessary feature qualifying something or someone for inclusion in a group	correct ☐ incorrect ☐
Criteria is the plural form of criterion	correct ☐ incorrect ☐

2 Look at the concordances and list some *adjectives* that are commonly used before **criteria/criterion**. Group them according to what they tell about the criteria. (The first in each group has been done for you.)

Group 1 (type/quality)	Group 2 (subject area)	Group 3 (quantity)
clear criteria	*medical* criteria	*several* criteria
_____ criteria	_____ criteria	_____ criteria
_____ criteria		_____ criteria
_____ criteria		_____ criterion
_____ criteria		_____ criterion
_____ criteria		

3 Which *prepositions* are most commonly used after **criteria/criterion**?

_____   _____

Part 3: Criteria

Study these concordances, underlining or highlighting the central group of words that stand alone, as has been done in the first example. Then answer the questions which follow. You may like to look at question 1 before you start. (Remember -- just familiarise yourself with the key words.)

Group 1

```
rply from the profane, They had no clear criteria to show where the line was to be drawn. What carri
own some, though not all, of the medical criteria for determining sex, and resolves that these crite
cular facts. Obviously, purely objective criteria such as the patient's age or the particular illnes
ave to do is to come up with some set of criteria which relate to the relative value we are prepared
ged. <p> We can only identify the proper criteria correctly if we accept that medical treatment in g
e the biological criteria. Psychological criteria are thus given no weight, despite the fact that th
g pus cells in the urethra, but the same criteria cannot be applied to the woman. One is left with e
        partners. <p> Darwin used several criteria for distinguishing sexual characteristics selected
ical issue, and decides that, of all the criteria involved, the crucial ones for determining how the
essentially heterosexual character', the criteria used to assess 'womanhood' must, Ormrod J. asserts
concern here, what are important are the  criteria whereby resources are allocated. These have to be
ed above, 'I have not contended that the  criteria of excellence lack a rational basis in everyday li
of religious knowledge and provided the  criteria for distinguishing truth from heresy. Martin Luthe
countries would meet either of these two criteria, and that the total resources needed would be abou
```

Group 2

```
through some sign and whether we have a criterion by which we may recognise the sign and judge what
be evaluated. They do not have an agreed criterion of perfection that can be used as a principle for
mselves'; when they say that there is no criterion of truth, 'they are not speaking of what things a
many people, can in fact be taken as one criterion for human maturity. And such behaviour must of co
es, with few intermediates. The relevant criterion is whether two forms commonly interbreed in the w
used for the list of accepted books. The criterion for admission was not so much that traditions vin
role of sensory experience. For him the  criterion of musical phenomena was not mathematics but the
n Chapter 1. Is there such a thing as a 'criterion' of truth? Do we have any 'instrument' or means o
```

FIG. 5.6. Sample material: Criteria. Reprinted from *Exploring Academic English* (pp. 72–73), by J. Thurston and C. N. Candlin, 1997, with permission from the National Centre for English Language Teaching and Research (NCELTR), Australia. © Macquarie University.

Type of description	Focus of the description	Perspective of language	Research activities in ESP	Instructional activities in ESP
Speech acts	How speakers and writers use language to achieve their communicative purposes. An example of a speech act is making requests.	Language is seen in terms of a set of intentions of the individual.	Identification of the speech acts critical to participation in the target environment and of learners' difficulties with these acts.	Highlighting which speech acts the learners will need and the linguistic exponents that can be used to realise them
Genres	How members of discourse community typically format texts in response to communicative demands in workplace, professional or academic contexts. An example of an academic genre is the end of term paper.	Language is seen in terms of a set of conventionalised text types used by discourse communities. Although conventionalised, genres are understood to change and develop over time with new ones emerging in response to changing demands.	Identification of key genres in workplace, professional or disciplinary environments. Attempts to understand the expectations and values placed on these genres by those inside a discourse community and how language is used in relation to these values and expectations	Familiarising learners with the genres they will use in their target environments and helping them understand the values and expectations placed on them.
Social interaction	The means speakers and writers have of lubricating their discourse and making their language use appropriate. An example of a social interaction strategy is hedging	Language use is seen as strategic and the interest is placed on linguistic devices used by speakers and writers to establish and maintain good relations with others.	Identification of socially motivated strategies used in target workplace, professional and academic environments and their rationale.	Helping learners make their language use socially appropriate and highlighting the strategies speakers and writers use to frame their contributions to discourse in workplace, professional or academic environments.
Words with disciplinary specific meanings (and structures with specific disciplinary uses)	The concepts important for a discipline, workplace or profession. Examples are meanings associated with 'cost' in economics and the uses of conditionals in doctor-patient encounters.	Language is seen as the word and structure choices regularly made in specific disciplines, workplaces and professions and the concepts associated with these choices.	Identification of frequently used words or structures. Investigation of the collocations of words and the meanings they carry in that field and the uses of prevalent structures.	Helping learners express concepts in their fields. Focusing learners' attention on the linguistic environment of key words and highlighting key structures used in the target environment.

FIG. 5.7. Summary of types of description of language use.

2. Study a published course book oriented to one branch of ESP, such as English for Nurses or English for Academic Studies, to answer the following questions:
   - Is there evidence of a speech-act-based (functional) component to the syllabus and if so, how is it organized?
   - How realistic are the language exponents given for the various speech acts?
   - What additional information about the use of the speech acts in the target environment could usefully supplement the description presented in this course book?
3. Think of a group of ESP learners you may teach in the future. What written genres will they need in their target academic, workplace, or professional discourse community? Devise a set of interview questions that you could use to interview inside members of that community to identify the genres they deem to be important. The questions should aim to elicit views on the role the genres play, the communicative purposes they serve, and the expectations the discourse community has for them.
4. In what ways could you encourage your own ESP/EAP learners to investigate written genres in their specific fields?
5. How important is it to teach socially motivated strategies and formulas in ESP? In your opinion, are politeness strategies and hedging 'icing on the cake,' that is, nonessential items?
6. Conduct a small-scale project to identify the concepts associated with and use of important words in one specialist area by following these steps:
   - Establish a corpus of texts used in a target environment—for example, five texts written by members of one profession or academic discipline.
   - Identify five high frequency content words (nongrammar words) in the corpus.
   - Investigate how these words are used by examining the surrounding linguistic environment. Also investigate the shared frame of reference of the items (the concepts these words carry in the target environment) by discussing them with inside members of the profession or discipline.

FURTHER READING

- Paltridge (2000) offers a general overview of different approaches to analysis of language use.
- Johns (2002) presents an edited volume containing a wide range of perspectives on genre analysis, reports of empirical studies into genres in

various contexts, and discussion of classroom applications of genre-based approaches to language description.

Articles illustrating the four different types of description examined in this chapter in relation to specific EAP and ESP contexts are as follows:

- Crandall and Basturkmen (2004) report on a study to evaluate the effectiveness of using speech-act-based materials in an EAP teaching context.
- A study by Parks (2001) examines the ability of employees to learn work-related genres. Parks compared care plans written by Francophone nurses studying in universities in Quebec with those written subsequently when the nurses were employed in an English-medium hospital in Montreal.
- Silver's (2003) study examines how writers in history and economics use hedging and other means to achieve an appropriate stance and to position themselves in relation to their respective academic communities.
- White (2003) examines meanings and metaphors associated with the word 'growth' in economics texts.
- Willis (1998) proposes activities teachers and students can use to work with corpora and concordances without a computer (well worth consulting if you are attempting item 6 in the preceding section).

This page intentionally left blank

Chapter 6

Combining Language Descriptions

Chapters 4 and 5 examined different types of language description in ESP. These were described in isolation to illustrate their specific characteristics. Although some ESP teaching or research may rely on one type of description, many ESP courses of instruction or research projects involve a combination or combine descriptions of language with a focus on language skills. The aim of this chapter is to illustrate this. Three examples are used: an extract of in-house teaching material developed for engineering students at Kuwait University, a course outline from a published work on academic speaking, and a report of a research study that investigated language use in a factory setting in New Zealand.

IN-HOUSE TEACHING MATERIAL
FOR ENGINEERING STUDENTS

Genre-based language description

+

Grammar

Figure 6.1 shows part of a set of teaching materials developed for engineering students over a number of years by teachers working in the English Language Unit in the Faculty of Engineering and Petroleum at Kuwait University. This material is taken from the first part of the English 221 course. This part of the course aims to help the students write abstracts for reports on engineering projects that involve innovative procedures, techniques, or designs.

English 221 aims to help students develop their ability to write technical texts. It is a Stage 2 course for mixed classes of undergraduate students

INTRODUCTION TO THE ABSTRACTING UNIT

Abstracting is a complex art. It involves a number of different skills which, when taken individually, are difficult and which, when combined, are very demanding indeed: reading with understanding; extracting relevant information; reorganizing that information according to a given purpose; and combining the reorganized information in a way which is grammatical, coherent, cohesive and concise. Do not underestimate the difficult nature of what you are being asked to do.

STUDENT OBJECTIVES: ABSTRACTING UNIT

By the time you finish the abstracting unit, you should be able to do the following:

1. read and understand various texts from periodical literature related to engineering and science;

2. understand how ideas are linked within and among paragraphs in articles and how these links affect organization;

3. write logical, cohesive, concise, thematically accurate and balanced summaries (abstracts) of articles from periodical literature and readings from other texts.

The abstracts that you write in this unit will be graded according to the following criteria:

1. All main ideas are present.

2. Your presentation is:

    2.1. concise
    2.2. coherent (Organization is logical, not necessarily following
                 the organization of the original text.)
    2.3. cohesive
    2.4. grammatically accurate/intelligible/stylish

FIG. 6.1.   Introduction to the abstracting unit. (This material is the production of teachers at the ELU Engineering Language Centre, Kuwait University.)

1.1. Title

Every abstract you write in this course must have a title. The title for the abstract will be the same as the title of the article. The title will be centered and capitalized correctly. (See student abstract sample, page 4.)

1.2. Thesis Sentence

The first sentence of every abstract is the thesis sentence. The thesis sentence is always ONE sentence. This sentence informs the reader of the subject, purpose and emphasis of the article.

In order to decide what information to include in the thesis sentence, ask yourself why this article was written. This will help you find the correct emphasis and focus your ideas. One good way to do this is to place key words or phrases in the thesis sentence. These words or phrases will let you and the reader know how you are going to discuss the topic and where the emphasis in the abstract will lie.

For example, students often say the article, "Adobe: A Possible Solution for the World's Building Problems," is about adobe. However, the article was not written because of adobe. It was written because of a new development: an adobe-block-making machine. Without the development of the machine, the article would not have been written. The focus of the thesis sentence, then, is the machine.

(incorrect)   Adobe is an old building material which may be used today to solve the world's housing problems.

(correct)   An adobe-block-making machine has been invented as a possible solution to the world's housing shortage.

As you can see from the incorrect example above, the thesis sentence only focuses on adobe and the housing problem, leading the reader to believe that the article discusses only these two points. Since the purpose of the thesis sentence is to inform the reader of the scope of the article, i.e. solution in this case, the above-mentioned thesis sentence is incorrect or at least incomplete.

Before writing the thesis sentence, answer these questions:

1. Why was the article written?
   What does the writer want to tell us?
2. Does the article describe a solution to a problem?
3. Does the article describe a device, a method, a process, a system, a technique, a plan or a new product?
4. What does it do? (its purpose)
5. Where? (include this if it is important)

FIG. 6.1 *(continued)*

The verb in the thesis sentence is important. The tense informs the reader if the article is about something which has already been developed, is presently being developed or will be developed in the future. Although other verb tenses may be used in certain articles in this course, the most common tenses are listed below.

Present perfect	$\Rightarrow$	has been developed
Present progressive	$\Rightarrow$	is being developed
Future	$\Rightarrow$	will be developed
		may be developed

The choice of verb also informs the reader of important information. When choosing the verb for the thesis sentence, consider what the emphasis in the article is. Does the article describe something which:

has been developed
is being used
will be marketed
may be introduced?

REMEMBER:

* The purpose of the thesis sentence is to inform the reader of the scope (i.e., the subject and purpose) of the article.

* Placing key words or phrases in the thesis sentence tells the reader where the emphasis in the abstract will lie.

* A thesis sentence with the correct emphasis helps focus the writer's ideas.

* Use the correct verb tense.

EXAMPLES:

A new water sterilization system will soon be tried out on a French town as an alternative to adding chlorine.

A prelubricating device has been invented which reduces wear caused by starting a car before the engine is lubricated.

An early warning device has been developed which indicates dangerous levels of stress in large structures.

A computerized plant dehydration detection system has been developed to determine farmers' and fruit growers' irrigation needs.

FIG. 6.1 *(continued)*

studying for degrees in civil, chemical, petroleum, computer, electrical, and mechanical engineering. Students are admitted to this second-stage course on successful completion of elementary and first-level English language courses provided by the university. English 221 focuses on writing abstracts and recommendation proposals, two written genres that are understood to be important in engineering.

English 221 is a course about written language. It does not focus on writing processes. It does not focus on skills development, although reading and writing practice are involved. To produce an abstract, writers need first to extract relevant information from a text (a reading skill) before reorganizing it (a writing skill). As these and other skills are practiced in the course, the students hopefully develop them. The course, however, does not set out in any deliberate or systematic way to foster the development of these skills. The main focus of the course is on features of the two written genres (how abstracts and recommendation reports are typically organized and what kind of content they contain).

Two types of language description are offered in the course and this can be seen in the representative sample of material shown in Fig. 6.1. The main description offered is genre-based. Instruction is organized around two genres, the abstract and the recommendation report. It aims to raise students' awareness of the kind of content typically found in these genres and how it is organised in engineering.

The material in Fig. 6.1 first introduces students to the notion of abstracting. Then it highlights the first move in abstracts. This move is labeled the 'thesis statement.' The move is described in relation to its communicative purpose (to explain why the article was written and its scope). Materials following on from those shown in Fig. 6.1 focus on subsequent moves in abstracts.

In terms of procedure, the students read a description of the thesis statement (and the article from which the statement was drawn—an article reporting a project to manufacture adobe bricks for building). The material highlights the purposes of the thesis statement and its linguistic features—including the use of words such as device, method, and process—and verb phrases.

The verb phrase section marks a transition to a description of grammar. The material contrasts the form and meaning of the present perfect passive 'has been developed' with the present progressive passive 'is being developed.' Information is given about the use of these forms in general. Genre-based approaches to language description often proceed from examination of the purpose and positioning of moves in a genre to analysis of grammar or vocabulary use in those moves (for example, see Swales, 1990). However, this differs from the approach evident in the teaching material just described. The approach used by Swales and genre analysts generally is descriptive and is concerned with the choice of grammatical forms or vocabulary in relation to the communicative purposes of the move and the genre. The information about verb tenses presented in the material earlier is prescriptive and describes verb tenses in the abstract as part of the grammar system.

The material shown in Fig. 6.1 progresses from description of the structure of the genre (the first move in the abstract) to a focus on grammatical aspects of verb tenses in general. As the course is organized around two genres, it can best be described as genre-based. As the course involves some general content on grammatical forms in English and their uses, it can be described as offering some (limited) description of English grammar as well.

AN ACADEMIC SPEAKING COURSE

Speaking-skills-focused course
+
Speech-act-based language description

Figure 6.2 shows a course outline (referred to as a 'Language Help Overview') taken from a published course book. The book offers skills practice and development. It is divided into topical units including Health and Education. There is a skills focus, and the course covers skills involved in giving presentations (looking for ideas to shape a talk, giving an overview, and rehearsing) and participating in discussions.

In addition, the course offers some language description of a number of speech acts important to participation in academic speaking including expressing opinions, asking questions, and asking for clarification. In the work, a range of possible realizations for these acts are presented. Realizations such as: I'm afraid I didn't follow your point about . . . Could you go over that again? Could you explain what you meant when you said that . . . ? Could you expand a little on what you said about . . . are presented for the act of asking for clarification.

RESEARCH STUDY INTO WORKPLACE LANGUAGE

Speech-act-based language research
+
Investigation of aspects of social interaction

A study by Pascal Brown (2001) described language use in a tanning factory in New Zealand. The study was speech act based. The main speech act

TABLE OF UNITS

UNIT	TOPIC	SKILLS FOCUS	LANGUAGE HELP
Foundation	You and your course	Exchanging information	Repair expressions
1	Countries	Preparing a presentation	Asking questions after a presentation
2	The home	Preparing for your audience	Describing an object
3	Education	Looking for ideas to shape your talk	Signpost expressions
4	The family	Collecting information	Comparison and contrast Describing trends
5	The media	Giving an overview	Asking for clarification
6	Health	Preparing a group presentation	Expressing proportion
7	Population and migration	Responding to questions	Describing trends Cause and effect Responding to questions
8	Defence	Generating ideas	Expressing opinion Agreeing and disagreeing
9	Parapsychology	Rehearsing and evaluating	Referring to a text Expressing opinion
10	Studying in a new environment	Summarising in discussion	Deduction

FIG. 6.2. Language help overview. From *Speaking Student's Book* (p. vii), by M. Rignall and C. Furneaux, 1997, Hemel Hempstead: Prentice Hall. Reprinted by permission of Pearson Education Ltd.

targeted for investigation was directives. Directives were identified in line with Holmes (1983) as acts to try to get others to do things. The study was interested in how workers and key figures in the factory, such as the manager, the foreman, and the accountant, used directives. It was motivated in part by concerns to prepare non-English speakers for work in factory settings in New Zealand and recognition that following (and giving) directives are a key speech act in this workplace context. It involved study of who used directives and when. It also involved examination of the syntactic choices the speakers used (declaratives, interrogatives, and statements) in making directives in the factory setting.

Data was collected from a number of participants who carried clip-on microphones attached to their clothing. These devices self-activated when conversation started in the vicinity of the participants and recorded the naturally occurring talk between the key participants and others in the factory. From the recordings, Pascal Brown identified directives (attempts by the speaker to get the hearer to do something). Once the researcher had identified and listed the directives each participant made, the participants were presented with the list and asked to check that these utterances had indeed been intended as directives. In this way, Pascal Brown was able to collect a data set of approximately 300 directives made in the factory.

The data set was then analyzed for the following features:

1. The choice of syntactic forms by the participants.
2. The relationship between the forms selected by the participants, strength of the directives, and the power relationships and social distance between the speakers.
3. The use of modifying devices (hedges or other means to minimize or maximize the strength of the directives) by the participants.

The primary focus of the study was on speech acts (directives) and the relationships between social factors (such as status and distance) and the language choices made by the people working in the factory. It also involved a focus on social interaction and hedging.

SUMMARY

Different types of language description are often merged in instruction in ESP and ESP oriented research. Often it is the case that one type of description predominates. The first example (the material developed for engineering students) illustrated genre-based instruction supported with some grammar focus and practice in writing and reading skills. The second example illustrated a course based mainly on speaking skills but that involved description of speech acts. The final example illustrated research into a particular speech act and involved investigation of social factors and a feature of social interaction, hedging.

QUESTIONS FOR DISCUSSION AND PROJECTS

1. Choose a published ESP or EAP course book. Examine the book's front matter (Table of Contents, Outline, and Introduction) to identify types of language description provided. Also examine a sample chapter from the book. Does any one type of language description predominate?
2. One of the arguments against a genre-based approach to writing instruction in general is that it can lead to a prescriptive approach in which students' creativity is hampered (Badger & White, 2000). Do you agree? Is ESP an area of teaching where a prescriptive approach is justified in any case?
3. Do you agree with the view that all ESP courses, regardless of their level or specific orientation, should offer some description of English grammar?
4. Survey the language-focused research studies in one volume of an ESP-oriented journal (for example, English for Specific Purposes or English for Academic Purposes Journal). Identify which types of language description are provided in the work.
5. Select a written text or transcript of a spoken text that would be of interest to an ESP class you teach or may teach in the future. How could you use the same text to present two different types of language description?

FURTHER READING

- Weber (2001) argues the case for EAP writing instruction combining concordances and genre-based approaches. Weber illustrates this combination with reference to a course in legal essay writing for undergraduate students of law.
- Badger and White (2000) discuss the strengths and weaknesses of product, process, and genre-based writing programs and propose an approach informed by all three approaches.
- Pascal Brown and Lewis (2002) report a study that followed on from the language-based research described earlier. The report of their study discusses how teachers can use computer software to analyze authentic samples of oral work-place language and how teachers can use such analyses in teaching preemployment ESP courses.

This page intentionally left blank

SECTION B

Learning

This page intentionally left blank

Chapter 7

Conditions for Learning

Chapters 7 and 8 examine links between theories about language learning and ESP. Although explicit discussion of learning has been limited in the ESP literature (see chapter 1), ideas about learning can be inferred from the course and materials designs developed and the types of research undertaken. This chapter is concerned with ideas about the conditions needed in order for language learning to take place. Chapter 8 concerns the processes through which learning is understood to occur.

This chapter examines two ideas about conditions needed for language learning and how these ideas are reflected in ESP teaching and research. The first idea (acculturation) is based on social considerations and is premised on the idea that ESP learners need to be in close social proximity or contact with their target discourse communities. The second idea (input and interaction) is based on linguistic considerations and rests on the argument that provision of sufficient linguistic input and opportunities for interaction are prerequisites for language learning.

ACCULTURATION

Concepts

Some ESP courses strive to provide access for their students to their target workplace, academic, or professional environments (these will be referred to as *target discourse communities* in the remainder of this chapter). The premise behind this endeavour is that access enables learners to become socially and psychologically integrated into their target discourse community and that this kind of integration is necessary for learning the specific-purpose language.

A link between successful second-language learning and acculturation was proposed by Schumann (1986). Schumann was interested in uninstructed second-language learning and the question of why some learners fail to progress beyond initial language-learning stages. Schumann suggested that success or failure was linked to differences in the levels of social and psychological contact that the groups of second-language learners had with the target language group. He argued, "The degree to which a learner acculturates to the target language group will control the degree to which he acquires the second language" (p. 384).

A number of social and psychological factors were suggested by Schumann as impacting on the level of acculturation and thus success in learning.

Social

Power Relations Between the Two Groups. A learner will be more inclined to acquire the language of a group that is perceived as dominant, for example, a group that has economic influence over the learner's first language group. Dominance by the target language group is a more favorable condition for successful second-language learning than nondominance.

Desire to Assimilate. Learners are more likely to acquire the language of a group that they wish to integrate with than one from which they wish to remain distinct. The desire by the second-language learners to assimilate into the target language group is a more favourable condition for successful second language learning than the desire for preservation of a distinct identity.

Extent of Shared Facilities. Learners are more likely to acquire the language of a group with which they share amenities. High enclosure within the target language group is a more favorable condition for successful second language learning than low enclosure.

Psychological (Language and Culture Shock). Learners are more likely to be successful in learning the second language if they are familiar with the second language and with the culture of the second-language speakers.

Research

Kirkgoz (1999) reports on a research project she conducted as part of her work teaching English for Academic Purposes to students at an English-medium university in Turkey. The students were on a 1-year pre-university English-language program. They had been accepted into various departments in the university but in line with university policy were required to complete one year's study of English and pass a proficiency examination as a prerequisite to actually starting courses in their departments. Normally, the 1-year intensive English-language study program is an English for General Academic Purposes course. Students who will study in different departments in the university are taught in mixed classes. The instruction does not involve, usually, attempts to create closer contact between the students studying in the English Language program and the departments in which they will study later on. Normally, the focus is on general academic language and skills.

The study aimed to investigate whether studying in a program geared toward acculturation led to better learning of English. The study wanted to find out if students with more social contact with their target discourse culture and language use in it would have more success in learning the language. The research set about 'acculturating' students into their target discourse communities while simultaneously offering them English for Specific Academic Purposes instruction, to study the effects of this on the students' learning of English.

The research participants were students who were to study in the Department of Economics and Business the following year. The students were divided into two groups. One group of students was the control group. They followed the usual curriculum of English for General Academic Purposes in the intensive 1-year English language program. The second group was the treatment group. They were 'acculturated' into their target discourse community. The treatment included a number of acculturation-oriented interventions:

1. The treatment group was formed into a replica discourse community (RDC—that is, a replica of the target discourse community). The idea behind this was to enable the learners to feel they were already part of a group related to the target discourse community. A special EAP class was formed consisting only of students who were to study in the Department of Economics and Business the next year.

2. The RDC group members were given a program in which they were required to periodically attend the lectures held in the Department of Economics and Business. The aim was for the students to share amenities with those already in the target discourse community and have increased social contact with them.

3. EAP instruction for the RDC group included content from Economics and Business studies. This took the form of introducing disciplinary concepts and vocabulary, such as 'scarcity' and 'opportunity cost.'

The study examined the combined effects of these treatments on the students' learning. The students' examination results in economics and business studies after their first year of study in their departments showed that the treatment group members outperformed the control group members.

The results of the study seem to indicate that students who had more social and psychological contact with the target discourse community, the Department of Economics and Business, were more successful than those who had more limited contact. The teacher/researcher had set up favorable conditions for learning for her EAP students. She had increased their contact with their target department in the university and created a replica discourse community so that psychologically the EAP class functioned to give the students a sense of belonging to a specialist discourse community.

Applications

A number of ESP instructional practices are designed to familiarize learners with the language practices of target discourse communities. But is it enough for ESP students to learn this from the outside and simply emulate practices? Or do they need to integrate with those communities? Do they need to understand the mind-set of those carrying out the practices and discover what Benson (1994) refers to as the "structures, values, norms, and procedures of that culture, which may or may not parallel his or her background knowledge from the first language environment" (p. 192).

The remainder of this section discusses the topic of acculturation in relation to genre-based approaches to ESP. In line with Swales (1990), genres are understood to signal a discourse community's norms and ways of thinking and constructing knowledge. Wharton (1999) identifies three models of acculturation in relation to genre-based approaches in ESP:

Induction. The ESP course takes place prior to students gaining experience in the target discourse community. The ESP teacher explains the genres used in the target discourse community and their associated cultural values. The learners are offered opportunities to practice the genres in the language classroom. Learners may be informed also of criteria for good performance in the genres. Thus learning about and practice of the genres takes place in vitro.

Adjunct. ESP learners simultaneously participate in their target discourse community and take ESP courses. The ESP courses provide assistance with the genres the learners are meeting in situ. For example, the learners join in events in the target community while attending an ESP course. The ESP course provides the learners with explicit information about the genres they meet in these events. This information raises the learners' metacognition of the genres and informs them of the cultural values attached to the genre.

Apprenticeship or Mentoring. The ESP students learn genres primarily through direct experience in the target discourse community. ESP instruction is offered as support and mainly takes the form of linguistic assistance. The features of the genres and associated cultural values are learned in situ.

The induction model is common in ESP. Students learn about the forms of communications in the target discourse community in the classroom, with the ESP teacher providing information about genres or other features of communication in the target discourse communities and practice opportunities. Turner (1996) argues for genre-based classroom instruction using tasks designed to bring to students' conscious attention the value systems of the community behind the genres. The aim is for the students to learn not only the genre conventions (linguistic information), but also the ways of thinking and the belief systems of the community.

Although classroom-based second-language genre instruction is common, some writers question its usefulness as an approach. Wharton (1999) argues that students with experience of genres in their first language experience difficulties in acquiring the genre in a second language. Genres are associated with particular ways of thinking and value systems. The learners have already established ways of thinking and values associated with the genre and thus the second system can be experienced as conflicting with the original system. Cadman (1997) investigated the impact of instruction focused on teaching the 'thesis' genre to postgraduate second-language learners. Cadman found that the learners were perplexed by statements of criteria for writing in their disciplines. Although they could identify the desired characteristics in sample texts, they did not understand how they were to achieve them in their own writing.

The replica discourse community group in Kirkgoz' study (1999) represents an 'adjunct model.' The ESP teacher/researcher helped her students gain shared facilities and social contact with the target discourse community. Meanwhile the students had classroom-based ESP instruction (note that this instruction was not focused only on genre features).

The apprenticeship model can be seen in the study reported by Parks (2001). Parks investigated the on-the-job genre acquisition by a group of Francophone nurses of nursing care plans in English. Specifically, the study examined how the nurses came to acquire the written genre of nursing care plans as used in their place of work in an English-medium hospital in Montreal. The nurses had originally learnt this genre during their training in a French-medium university hospital in Quebec. The study found that differences emerged in the writing of the nurses principally in relation to their varying perceptions of the goals or motives for the genre in their workplace. However, the nurses were able to produce acceptable care plans from the start of their work experience mainly due to being part of the nursing community and the scaffolding that was available for them from colleagues and to their continual exposure to models of nursing care plans written by experienced Anglophone nurses around them. One of a number of suggestions made by Parks on the basis of her findings is that one role for the second-language 'consultant' is to sensitize learners to how to make better use of resources for help with communicative practices already available in the community of practice.

The induction model of genre-based ESP represents a weak version of acculturation theory. The learners are positioned on the outside of their target discourse communities as observers of the discourse practices and values of inside members. Through observation and emulation, it is expected that they will come to share the mind-set of the inside members. The adjunct model of ESP represents a stronger version of the theory. ESP instruction forges actual links between the ESP students and their target discourse communities, at the same time offering classroom-based instruction. The apprenticeship model represents the strongest version of the theory. The student learns to communicate in the discourse community by being a member of that community. The ESP instructor acts as a language consultant. The various versions of ESP discussed in this section have a common premise: Some form of integration between the ESP learners and their target discourse provides favorable conditions for language learning.

INPUT AND INTERACTION

Concepts

A second way ESP courses strive to provide favourable conditions for language learning is by their attempt to create an optimal linguistic environment, one in which learners are provided with plenty of input in the form of exposure to the target specialist language and opportunities for students to interact with it. Sufficient quantity and quality of linguistic input and interaction are understood to be conditions favourable for language learning.

The concepts of linguistic input and interaction as requisites for language learning can be traced historically to 'natural' methods in language teaching (Stern, 1992). They are seen in formal theories of second language acquisition that have emerged over the years. Krashen's *Input Hypothesis* (1982) proposed that learners acquire language by understanding messages intelligible to them. They learn by being exposed to sufficient 'comprehensible input,' that is, input that is slightly above their level of immediate comprehension. The latter was referred to as I (interlanguage) +1. Comprehensible input of the I +1 variety has the potential to become 'intake' (learning). Long (1996) developed Krashen's *Input Hypothesis*, arguing that learning occurs not because of input alone, but also through the interaction learners have with it. Long's Interaction Hypothesis can be summarized as:

1. Learners can only learn what they are ready to learn (they have their own internal syllabus).
2. Linguistic input is necessary for learning.
3. Learners negotiate the meaning of input to make it more comprehensible to themselves.
4. Through negotiation of meaning, the input becomes increasingly useful because it is targeted to the specific developmental level of the individual learner.
5. Thus input negotiated to fit the needs of the individual learner can become intake.

The original hypothesis was later developed by Long to include a role for corrective feedback. Long (1996) argues that negative feedback obtained during negotiation of meaning contributes to acquisition (at least for vocabulary, morphology, and language-specific syntax, and L1–L2 contrasts). Input provides samples of positive evidence of how the language system operates or how language is used. Explicit negative evidence such as corrections or implicit negative feedback, including 'recasts' (reformulations by another speaker of the same message but with improved language), can provide learners with information they need to notice the gap between their own output and target language forms.

It has also been argued that the level of attention learners pay to the input in the language environment plays a role in intake, that is, a language form or use is incorporated into the learner's developing second language in relation to the level of conscious attention the learner pays to it (Schmidt, 1994; Sharwood Smith, 1993). Schmidt argues that "more noticing leads to more learning" (p. 18). According to these writers, learners need to notice (but not necessarily be consciously aware of) language features in order for acquisition to occur. The implications for instruction of these ideas is that teaching needs to raise the saliency of language features (forms, routines, and patterns) in order for learners to notice them. This can be done through input enhancement or consciousness raising activities.

Research

The interaction hypothesis has led to attempts to identify the types of learning activities or tasks that are more likely to create the conditions for extensive negotiation of meaning. For example, a study by Pica, Young, and Doughty (1987) found that learners who were allowed to ask questions about a written text had better comprehension of it than those who did not but read a simplified version of the text.

Robinson, Strong, Whittle, and Nobe (2001) conducted an experiment to assess the effect of a task-based approach on the development of EAP oral discussion skills. In the study, three groups of learners were taught discussion skills on a weekly basis over a one-semester period using different teaching methods:

Group 1
Task-based method (exposure to input and interaction).

Group 2
Structured focus on form comprising task-based method (exposure to input and interaction) + teacher-led posttask noticing (awareness-raising) activities.

Group 3
Traditional skill-based method consisting of learners being taught a series of academic discussion microskills, for example, phrases for agreeing and disagreeing and rules for turn taking.

Scores on tests after the teaching period showed that learners from Groups 2 and 3 had similar scores and generally outperformed learners from Group 1. The result led the researchers to conclude that "structured focus on form, where teachers provide many activities for directing learner attention to aspects of their task performance that differ from native speaker norms, plus extensive whole task practice is equivalent to carefully targeted and sequenced micro-skills teaching" (pp. 357–358). It should be noted that the researchers point out that longer term studies of the effects of different kinds of task-based methods are needed.

Applications

Input and interaction hypotheses have also led to proposals for task-based language teaching. Tasks are devised that create conditions for negotiation of meaning with input. ESP has embraced task-based teaching alongside general ELT. Tasks are defined as pieces of work in everyday life with a specific objective, such as painting a fence, filling in a form, making an airline reservation. They are nonlinguistic units.

Jasso-Aguilar (1999) argues that task-based, as opposed to text-based, units of analysis are required for needs analysis and course design in ESP, and that members of target discourse communities can be called on to explain the tasks:

Task is a more relevant and viable unit of analysis, since more relevant information is available in task-based occupational analyses from domain experts

and other sources; task-based analyses reveal more about the dynamic quali-
ties of target discourse than do text-based analyses, and they also circumvent
the domain expert's lack of linguistic knowledge and the applied linguist's
lack of content knowledge. . . . Once the target tasks have been identified,
domain experts (not necessarily the learners, unless they have expertise) can
easily and reliably supply information which will later be analysed by applied
linguistics, materials writers, teachers. (p. 30)

As discussed in chapter 3, in ESP, task-based syllabuses are equated with
use of tasks replicating real-world pieces of work (Lynch & Maclean, 2000).
The development of task-based syllabuses needs to be based on investigation
of the real-world tasks the learners will undertake in their target workplace
or academic or professional environments. According to Long and Crookes
(1992), the design of task-based syllabuses for ESP needs to include:

- Identification of target tasks (target situation tasks).
- Breaking the tasks down into target task types (subtasks/tasks within
  the task).
- Development of pedagogical tasks.
- Assessment of students by task-based criteria—as established by
  experts in their field, not language.

The difficulty of the task or subtask (how many steps are involved, how
many participants, their roles, and the intellectual difficulty) is related
to the nature of the task in the real world, rather than conventional
linguistic criteria. During task completion when students are focused on
expressing or comprehending meaning, 'pedagogical tasks' may be used
to draw students' attention to aspects of the language system or features of
language use.

A task-based academic speaking course was developed at a university in
New Zealand as part of an English for General Academic Purposes program
developed for students from a range of disciplines in the university. The
course is organized around three tasks:

1. Presentation by individual students of factual, literature-based information. Students research and then present definitions of two related
concepts or terms from their own subject of study. For example, a student
of political science might choose the terms 'autocracy' and 'monarchy.'

2. Presentation by groups of students of a research-based study. Students
conduct and then report on a survey study, such as student parking problems at the university.

3. Reporting new information and explanation of a process. Students
read an article reporting a recent technical innovation. They then explain

this innovation to a small group and lead a group discussion on it. For example, a student interested in environmental issues selects an innovation to use plants to detoxify radioactive emissions in nuclear power plants.

Each task is broken down into subtasks roughly representing how the task would need to be approached in an academic environment. For example:

> Task 2: Students conduct a survey and report on the results of the survey.
>   Subtasks
>   1. Decide on a research question for the survey.
>   2. Design data collection instrument (items for either a questionnaire or structured interview).
>   3. Pilot the instruments in class to get feedback on the items.
>   4. Collect data.
>   5. Collate and analyze data.
>   6. Design presentation report and visuals.

Pedagogical tasks were developed in relation to the subtasks. For example, the stage 'design data collection instrument' involves a task to raise students' awareness of language use in interviews. The class listens to a recorded interview and is led in analysis of question formation and strategy use.

Finally, students present their survey reports and are evaluated according to task-referenced criteria including their ability to report numerical information, relate conclusions to findings, and design visuals. A sample task specification sheet from this course is shown in Fig. 7.1.

SUMMARY

This chapter examined attempts in ESP to create the conditions in which successful language learning is thought to occur. The first attempt concerned research and teaching focused on reducing the social and psychological distance between ESP learners and members of their target discourse communities. The second attempt concerned research into task-based instruction and teaching focused on tasks replicating the kinds of work the ESP students will do in their target discourse communities. Figure 7.2 shows a summary of the ideas discussed in this chapter. In the figure, TCD refers to target discourse community.

QUESTIONS FOR DISCUSSION AND PROJECTS

1. To what extent do you use real-world tasks in your own teaching? What are some of the advantages and disadvantages of this?

Survey Project (30%)

The Task
To conduct a small-scale survey and present the results and conclusions from it.

1. Preparation of Questionnaire (work with partner)

- select an area of research, eg. students' use of the library, reasons for choosing economics as a course of study, etc.
- determine the focus of the research - the main research question and 3 sub-questions related to it.
- devise a short questionnaire of 5 to 10 items,
- trial the questionnaire in class session & refine as necessary
- questionnaire to be typed and photocopied
- administer the questionnaire to 10+ respondents

2. Analysis of Data

- tabulate data
- analyse data & draw conclusions from it

3. Presentation
(individual work)

- prepare outline of the presentation & visuals
- presentation to last from 6 to 10 minutes
- presentation to be given **using outline only** (not written notes)
- outline to include:

Introduction (overall aim of research, main divisions & sample population)

Findings related to sub-question 1
Findings related to sub-question 2
Findings related to sub-question 3

Conclusions drawn from findings

- Present a report of the survey and respond to audience questions.

FIG. 7.1.   Task specification worksheet from an academic speaking course.

2. How feasible is it for you to obtain access for your ESP classes to their target discourse communities? What kind of access do you see as desirable and what practical steps might help you obtain it?
3. Do you think teachers of preexperienced ESP classes should preferably be members (or former members) of the target discourse communities? Why or why not?
4. Wharton (1999) reports that students with experience of genres in their first language experience conflicts when learning those genres

Theory	Conditions	Teaching Strategies	Research Example
Acculturation	Social	Aim to reduce the social and/or psychological distance between ESP learners and TCDs	Kirkgoz (1999) investigated the effects of levels of contact between language learners and TCDs on learning
Input and interaction	Linguistic	Aim to provide exposure to language use and engage learners in tasks replicating work in the TCD	Robinson et al. (2001) investigated the effects of task types on learning

FIG. 7.2.   Conditions for learning ESP.

in a second language. Have you experienced such conflicts in learning genres or observed them in your teaching?

5. Parks (2001) suggests that a prime role for the on-site second-language consultant is to raise learners' awareness of the resources for help with communicative practices that are already available in the workplace. List practical steps a language consultant in a hospital setting (such as that in which Parks conducted her research) could take to do this.

FURTHER READING

- Johns (1997b) describes a linked (adjunct) model of EAP in a U.S. university setting.
- Chapter 6 in Mitchell and Myles' book *Second Language Learning Theories* (1998) provides a useful survey of theories and empirical research on input and interaction in second-language learning.
- A detailed account of Schumann's acculturation model can be found in Schumann (1978).
- Comparison of task-based syllabus designs in ESP and ELT are described in Long and Crookes (1992).
- Ellis (2003) explores the relationship between research and task-based teaching and course designs.

Chapter 8

Processes of Learning

The previous chapter examined ideas about the conditions needed for learning and made links between such ideas and ESP teaching and research. However, language learning does not only occur because learners enjoy conditions favourable to learning. It occurs also as a result of learners engaging in cognitive processes and mental activities. This chapter examines the links between ESP teaching and research and theories in the Second Language Acquisition literature.

Perspectives about learning processes can be divided into two explanations—intermental and intramental. The former explains language learning as resulting from the cognitive processes of the individual learner, and the latter as resulting from the social activity of the learner (Mitchell & Myles, 1998). This chapter examines two theories of language learning as a process: information processing (an intramental perspective) and activity theory (an intermental perspective of learning). It also examines the content-based approach to language teaching and ESP, an approach that can be linked to information processing perspectives of learning.

INFORMATION PROCESSING

Concepts

Information processing construes language learning as a complex behaviour composed of simpler processes. Learning is seen as an incremental process. The processes take time and practice. Through practice, there is development from controlled to automatic processing (McLaughlin & Heredia, 1996). This involves two types of memory and two stages of learning—controlled processing and automatization:

Controlled Processing. Learners attend to a selection of simple bits of information. This information is stored in the short-term memory. The amount of information that can be focused on at any one time is limited because of the limitations of the short-term memory.

Automatization.   The simple bits of information in the short-term memory are repeatedly activated through practice, and by this process they come to be stored in the long-term memory. From here, they can be automatically accessed rapidly with minimal effort. Once stored in the long-term memory, they become automatic. Then the learner is freed up and can move onto other bits of information and higher levels of processing, such as the integration of groups of information enabling complex language behavior (McLaughlin, 1987). According to Cook (1997), for teaching, the main application of processing models of acquisition is the role given to practice. The classroom can be seen as functioning to provide opportunities for students to practice what they have learnt so that what they have learnt becomes automatic.

Declarative and Procedural Knowledge

Anderson (1980) argues that information processing also involves the development of declarative and procedural knowledge. Declarative knowledge is 'knowledge that' (explicit knowledge). Through repeated activation, declarative knowledge becomes procedural knowledge or 'knowledge how.' We first learn the rules, and these are stored in our short-term memory. In time, these come to be stored in our long-term declarative memory and finally in our procedural long-term memory. From here they can be accessed rapidly and automatically:

> When we learn a foreign language in a classroom situation, we are aware of the rules of the language, especially after a lesson that spells them out. One might argue that our knowledge of the language at that time is declarative. We speak the learned language by using general rule-following procedures applied to the rules we have learned, rather than speaking directly as we do in our native language. Not surprisingly, this knowledge is a much slower and more painful process than applying the procedurally encoded knowledge of our own language. Eventually, if we are lucky, we can come to know a foreign language as well as we know our native language. At that point, we often forget the rules of the foreign language. It is as if the class-taught declarative knowledge has been transformed into procedural form. (p. 224)

Research

Evidence supporting the role of declarative knowledge in language learning is provided by Muranoi (2000). Muranoi conducted a quasiexperimental study of students' learning of articles (a, an, the). The students were given a learning task targeting the use of articles. Following the task, differ-ent groups received debriefing sessions by the teacher. Students in one group were given explicit grammatical debriefings involving the provision of explicit rules for article use in English. Other students received only meaning-focused debriefings on the task. Following this, the students were tested on their use of articles. Test scores showed that learners in the group that had received the grammatical debriefings outperformed those groups who had not received explicit information.

Dhieb-Henia (2003) investigated the effectiveness of metacognitive strat-egy training for reading research articles in ESP teaching contexts. Reading strategy research shows that although students in second-language reading programs may be provided with instruction in reading strategies, they may fail to use the strategies because of a lack of awareness (metacognition) about why the strategies are needed, and where and when to use them. Dheib-Henia's study involved students of biology who were taking reading courses in two universities in Tunisia.

Students in the experimental group were given an introduction to the research article as a genre. The introduction focused on the discoursal, rhetorical, and syntactic features of the genre. They were also given meta-cognitive strategy training in their reading classes. The first hour of each 2-hour lesson was given over to explicit presentation and discussion of a reading strategy and the second hour to practicing the strategy in reading articles from biology journals. In the first half of the lessons, the students were trained in different reading strategies, such as skimming, search read-ing and scanning. They discussed a set of questions:

What is this strategy?
Why should it be learnt?
When should it be used?
How can the strategy be used?
Where should the reader look?
How can you evaluate the use of the strategy?

Students in the control group received the reading approach normally used in the local context. This involved the use of short reading texts, focus-ing on vocabulary and grammar in them and answering comprehension questions.

Both groups of students took pre- and postcourse tests. Some students also participated in a retrospection activity in which they were provided with records of their tests and asked to recall how they had carried out the read-ings. Both test results and evidence from the retrospective accounts provided evidence that presentation of explicit information about research articles and the metacognitive strategy training led to improvements in proficiency in reading research articles and increased familiarity with this genre.

By the end of the course, learners will be able to

1. take part in short exchanges to get or give information or confirmation

2. form and be able to follow exchanges involving complex elicitations and responses

3. manage exchanges in which there are communication breakdowns and inter-turn repair sequences

4. extend exchanges until a satisfactory outcome is achieved.

Each discourse skill is then broken down into micro-skills. For example:

2. Learners will be able to form and follow exchanges involving complex elicitation and responses by

forming elicits

supporting elicits with subsidiary acts

justifying elicits

using topic signalling devices in elicits

recognising topic signalling devices

identifying main and subsidiary discourse acts

identifying attitudinal features within elicits and responses

recognising extended patterns of elicitation

FIG. 8.1.   Discourse skills for academic speaking. Reprinted from *English for Specific Purposes,* Vol. 18, H. Basturkmen, "Discourse in MBA Seminars," pp. 63–80, Copyright © 1999, with permission from Elsevier Science.

Applications

Ideas about declarative knowledge and information processing are reflected in ESP instruction that focuses learners' attention on prespecified rules, routine, or strategies (often one at a time) followed by practice of those items. This is illustrated in the Discourse Skills for Academic Speaking syllabus shown in Fig. 8.1. The syllabus is specified as a list of discrete discourse skills.

This syllabus reflects the view that complex language behaviour is built on the accumulation of simple items or skills. For example, the students are introduced to topic signalling devices in elicits (questions). They are also shown extended patterns of elicitation. The students will eventually synthesize the discrete pieces of information and be able to perform the complex skill 'being able to follow exchanges involving elicitations.'

LEARNING THROUGH CONTENT

In content-based approaches to instruction (CBI), students are presented with discipline-based materials, and the main focus of instruction is the acquisition of disciplinary information (Kasper, 1997). Content-based approaches "view the target language largely as the vehicle through which subject matter content is learned rather than as the immediate object of study" (Brinton, Snow, & Wesche, 1989, p. 5). Wesche (1993) defines content-based instruction:

> Content-based language teaching is distinguished first of all by the concurrent learning of specific content and related language use skills in a 'content driven' curriculum, i.e. with the selection and sequence of language elements determined by content. . . . Essential to all content-based instruction is a view of language acquisition which emphasises the incidental internalisation of new knowledge by the learner from rich target language data, while focusing on meaning to be communicated. (pp. 57–58)

Proponents of content-based approaches draw on a range of theories in second language acquisition, including information processing and Anderson's (1983) Adaptive Control of Thought Theory in particular (Snow & Brinton, 1997). Snow and Brinton argue that depth-of-processing studies indicate that the presentation of coherent and meaningful information leads to deeper cognitive processing by the learner, which leads to better learning: 'Depth-of-processing research findings are consistent with CBI, an approach that, by definition, promotes extended study of coherent content and relevant language learning activities . . . depth-of-processing research provides support for the integration of language and content' (Snow & Brinton, 1997, p. 11).

Not all knowledge about language is explicit in origin. Rules and patterns may be acquired implicitly from the outset. Ellis (1997) argues that implicit knowledge is 'the default mode of cognition' (p. 113). The sheer volume of rules involved in learning a language suggests that language learning would be an impossible task if each rule and pattern had to be learnt as explicit information in the first place (Ellis, 1997). Like explicit knowledge, implicit knowledge can be acquired first through controlled and then through automatic processes. Implicit knowledge is acquired without awareness. A new implicit 'rule' that is first accessed slowly and inconsistently (controlled processing) is later used without effort (automatic processing). Explicit information is learnt consciously. This compares with explicit information learning. A new explicit 'rule' that is first used with deliberate effort (controlled processing) is later used with relative speed (automatic processing).

Research

The success of content-based approaches in ESP is reported in the literature. Parkinson (2000) reports on the advantages of a content-based approach to teaching English for science and technology in a South African University. Among the advantages noted by Parkinson were that the learners were able to build on their previous knowledge, were exposed to the contextualized uses of language, and were able to prepare for the eventual uses to which the language would be put. Hudson (1991) reports on the design and evaluation of effectiveness of a content-based approach to teaching reading English for science and technology at a university in Mexico. The course was organized around the course content in the students' undergraduate program and included topics such as energy and chemical engineering. Reading activities included tasks similar to those the students would actually perform in their undergraduate program. Hudson found the content-based approach resulted in significant improvement in the students' reading comprehension.

Kasper (1997) reviews research into the effects of content-based instruction to find that the studies have largely measured short-term effects. Kasper devised an experimental study to investigate the long-term effects of learning in a content-based course. The study involved two groups of students enrolled in ESL 09 (a four-semester intermediate level reading and writing course at a community college in the United States). The experimental group used a textbook of readings with selections from the five academic disciplines the students were most likely to study in the college. The students in the control group used a textbook of readings that covered a wide range of topic areas that were not grounded in any particular disciplinary areas. Instruction for both groups followed the same four-stage instructional sequence with each reading: a prereading stage introducing the topic and topic-related vocabulary and concepts; a factual reading stage in which students extrapolated information from the reading; a discussion and analysis stage in which the students synthesised the information they had gained from the readings to write summaries and expository essays; and a final extension activity, such as viewing a video on a related topic. Kasper compared the students' end-of-semester ESL 09 scores in a reading and writing proficiency test and also subsequent academic performance in mainstream English composition courses and their likelihood of graduating from the college with a degree. On all measures, Kasper found that the students who had received content-based ESL reading and writing instruction had significantly higher scores. The results indicated that content-based ESL instruction may have helped the experimental group members' subsequent performance in the college academic mainstream.

Applications

ESP makes extensive use of content-based approaches. According to Master and Brinton (1998), CBI has the following features. The syllabus is organised around subject content; for example, in a course for English for Economics students, the subject matter might be a number of topics from economics, such macroeconomics and supply and demand. Teaching activities are specific to the subject matter being taught and are geared to stimulate students to think and learn through the use of the target language. Language is viewed holistically, and learners learn from working with whole chunks of language and multiple skills. Content-based approaches reject 'synthetic' approaches to course design—the idea that language or skills can be atomized into discrete items to be presented and practiced by learners one at a time. The approach makes use of authentic texts to which learners are expected primarily to respond in relation to the content. It has been argued (Hutchinson & Waters, 1987) that once we remove the text from its original context, it loses some of its authenticity. For example, the intended audience is changed once the authentic text is imported into the classroom. Authenticity also relates also to the reader's purpose in reading the text. For example, recommendation reports for the purchase of technical equipment are, in their original context of use, devised for the purpose of helping the reader decide which of two or more items of equipment to buy. If, however, a recommendation report is transported into a language teaching classroom and students are given an activity whose purpose is to answer comprehension questions on it, the match between text and task is artificial. Content-based instruction tries to avoid some of these potential problems by using content (authentic texts) in ways that were similar to those in real life. Content-based approaches involve also the integration of skills. Writing often follows on from listening and reading, and students are often required to synthesize facts and ideas from multiple sources as preparation for writing (Brinton et al., 1989).

In short, the key features of CBI are:

1. Content is the organizing unit of course design.
2. Skills are integrated.

3. Language is approached holistically.

4. Extensive use of authentic texts.

Bishop-Petty and Engel (2001) report on a content-based approach used at the Defence Language Institute at San Antonio, Texas. This institute works with students who are experienced military personnel from a number of countries around the world. Previous attempts were made in the Institute to construct language courses based on a synthetic approach to language (the prespecification of language items to be presented and practiced one at a time), but these attempts were unsuccessful and have largely been replaced with a content-based approach.

To illustrate the content-based approach used and the view of learning underlying it at the Defence Language Institute, I outline one 'project' that the students work on during their program of English Language Instruction there. The project entails the students working on topics from their own specialist areas and making use of study guides collated by the language instructors. The guides are organized into subject areas within the students' specialist areas. For example, a military pilot might chose to work on the subject of air turbulence, a topic within 'aviation.'

To prepare the project, Bishop-Petty and Engel (2001) contacted air-force personnel to identify potential topics. For example, aviation personnel suggested topics such as air turbulence, aerodynamics, formation flying, air combat, and spatial disorientation. Having identified suitable topics, Bishop-Petty and Engel collected a wide range of reference sources (authentic readings, Web sites addresses, and articles) to form study guides for each topic.

The study guides consist of two parts:

Part 1. Resources
- Texts and references materials, such as an aircraft technical dictionary, a handbook on basic helicopter maintenance, aircraft manuals.
- Topics for impromtu talks and 'briefings' (formal presentations).

The texts are drawn from the actual work environment of the students. The topics for the briefings replicate the type of subjects students might be called to talk on in the target environment. For example, one briefing topic is: Discuss possible malfunctions of a fuel system and how the pilot should respond.

Part 2. Activities
- Authentic reading and listening texts with questions and vocabulary work sheets for self-study.

This section provides pedagogical rather than real-world tasks.

Students select a topic they want to work on, select materials from the resources and activities, and then use them to work on the language and prepare their briefings.

ACTIVITY THEORY—AN ECOLOGICAL PERSPECTIVE

Concepts

This chapter so far has concerned conceptualizations of learning as an individual activity, an activity in which learners mentally process language in order to acquire it. This section deals with a very different view—a view of learning as a social activity. Although sociocultural perspectives on learning are not new (a sociocultural perspective on learning was proposed by Vygotsky in the early 20th century), it is only fairly recently that the literature on language teaching has turned its attention to this subject. A number of Vygotsky's ideas have recently been taken up in the literature and applied to studies of second-language learning (Lantolf, 2000).

Discussion of sociocultural theory focuses on two central ideas. The first is the proposal that learning arises from and through social interaction. Learning is seen as, first, intermental (social) and then, second, as intramental (individual). Learning, therefore, is a two-stage process. For example, a learner is faced with a task he or she is unable to complete with his or her present knowledge and skills. However, the learner works on the task in collaboration with a more knowledgeable or skilful individual. That individual offers supportive dialogue to the learner as they work on the task together. By means of this supportive dialogue, the learner comes to share in the more expert individual's consciousness about how to complete the task. This supportive process is known as *scaffolding*. Learning is most productive if scaffolding is offered when the learner is in the Zone of Proximal Development (ZPD)—that is, the learner is nearly ready to function independently. Collaborative dialogic support from more capable individuals at this stage enables the learner to 'appropriate' (acquire) the concepts needed to do the task. As a result, the learner will be able to work independently on the task in the future (Mitchell & Myles, 1998).

A second idea is that learners actively construct their own learning environment. According to Mitchell & Myles (1998), social–cultural theorists reject transmission and computational models of learning in which learners receive or work on the language input they are provided with. They reject such models on the grounds that these models construe the learner as a passive recipient and what is learnt is determined by others, such as teachers and course designers. Such models construe teaching as providing input and learning as the taking in of input. In contrast, sociocultural theorists claim that learners shape their own learning, and they do so because they have their own individual goals. This perspective, known as *activity theory*, was developed by Leontiev, one of Vygotsky's successors.

Roebuck (2000) describes Leontiev's theory. Human activity is construed as a complex process, and the properties of any activity are seen as determined by the sociohistorical setting and by the goals and sociocultural history of the participants. Activity theory focuses on how individuals construct goals in unique ways and then carry out activities to achieve their own goals. In terms of language learning, this means that students play an important role in shaping the goals for and ultimate outcomes of tasks set for them by their teachers. So the key to understanding learning is to find out how individual learners have decided to engage with the task as an activity.

Van Lier (2000) proposes an ecological perspective on activity theory. He argues that the learner is immersed in an environment full of potential meanings and 'affordances,' and what the learner uses in this environment is dependant on what he or she wants and does. An affordance (for example, a leaf in the forest) offers different uses to different creatures in the forest. One creature may use the leaf for shade while another uses it for food. The properties of the leaf do not change, but different properties are perceived in it and acted on by different organisms. So in language learning, the same affordances will be perceived differently by different learners and used for different forms of linguistic actions. The affordances vary according to the different goals of the students, and what the students learn from the affordances in the language learning environment (for example, the classroom) varies also.

Van Lier's (2002) ecological view represents a major shift from an input–output view of learning to a view of learning as dependant on the quality of social interaction that occurs in the classroom. He argues that success from this perspective is judged on the quality of interaction between students and between teacher and students. Social interaction must be geared toward conversational symmetry. The task of the language teacher is 'to create learning opportunities for the students, to encourage them to be engaged, and to surround them with language experiences that can become affordances through meaningful social interaction' (p. 15).

Research and Applications

Studies based on activity theory have investigated how learners construct their own goals in instructed second-language learning. Donato (2000) reports the case of the same task being given by an ESL teacher to different groups of students in the one class. Each group interpreted the task differently. As a result, the task became a different activity for each group, and each group had a different goal and set about the task in different ways. Roebuck (2000) describes an experimental study in which students carried out a written recall task. The task required the students to write a report of newspaper articles in the second language. Some students oriented themselves to the goal of writing a report of the article, but others oriented themselves to using the task to understand the article themselves rather than to tell someone else about it.

As yet, the literature concerned with sociocultural perspectives in ESP is limited. One example is an exploratory study that investigated learner perspectives of success in an EAP writing course (Basturkmen & Lewis, 2002). Working from the perspective of activity theory, the study set out to examine how three students, in the same EAP writing course in a university setting in New Zealand, constructed success and their goals for studying academic writing. E-mail dialogues were set up between the researchers and the students to elicit the students' perceptions of what constituted success for them in the course, how successful they felt they were in their academic writing course, and what factors (for example, activities) they related their success to. The two teachers of the three students were also engaged in e-mail dialogues to elicit their perspectives of the three students and also which of the writing course objectives they emphasised in their teaching.

The study found that although there were some similarities in the students' constructs of success, there were mostly differences. For example, one student equated success largely with her growing ability to express her ideas in academic writing. Another equated success to her increased knowledge of academic writing conventions. This student had set out to meet the expectations of the academic community. The researchers found that although the three students had attended the same course with the same textbook and assignments (and, in the case of two students, had attended the same class with the same teacher), their interpretations of what constituted success was highly individual. This suggested that the students had pursued different objectives. The findings thus supported the premise of activity theory that the same activity means different things to different people.

SUMMARY

This chapter examined ideas about the processes by which language acquisition occurs. Information processing offered a view of learning as an individual mental activity. Advocates of content-based approaches argue that language is best learned through the process of learning disciplinary or technical subject content. Activity theory offered a sociocultural view of learning as a two-stage process—intermental and then intramental.

Activity theory also offered a view of learning as shaped and constructed by the goals of the learners. What would be the implications of this view for

ESP teaching? ESP has conventionally been centred on needs analysis and course design, with the often implicit assumption being made that what the ESP course teaches, the students will (all being well) learn—a computational view of learning; that is, teachers provide the input and students work on this to make it intake. However, activity theory suggests that it is the learners who determine what they will learn and the same instructional task or activity is typically used by different learners for different learning objectives, and thus that the students learn different things from them. ESP teachers accepting this position may need to rethink aspects of their traditional role in the classroom. For example, they would need to reorientate themselves away from being the providers of relevant input in the classroom and toward a role of scaffolding (that is, offering supportive dialogue) as they work alongside learners to complete language tasks.

QUESTIONS FOR DISCUSSION AND PROJECTS

1. How important is the presentation and subsequent practice of particular skills, strategies, or language items in your ESP teaching?
2. Dhieb-Henia (2003) investigated the effects of metacognitive strategy training in reading instruction. Do you know of other ESP courses that offer metacognitive strategy training? If so, what does the training involve?
3. To what extent do you expose your ESP class to content from various sources in their subject area? Would you describe your approach as content-based?
4. What objections might students and institutional representatives make if you tried to implement a purely content-based approach in your teaching situation? List arguments you could make to counter them.
5. Describe any experiences of scaffolding (as a teacher or learner) that you have experienced.
6. Basturkmen and Lewis (2002) investigated their learners' perspectives of success in an academic writing class. They corresponded with the students by e-mail to collect information. What learner perspectives might you like to investigate and how would you collect information?

FURTHER READING

- Concepts of explicit knowledge, implicit knowledge, controlled processing, and automatic processing are examined in Ellis (1997).
- Johns (1997a) discusses the relationship between ESP and content-based instruction.

- An introduction to the theoretical bases of content-based instruction and descriptions of content-based programs in a variety of settings are offered in Snow and Brinton (1997) and Brinton et al. (1989).
- Lantolf (2000) provides a collection of articles focusing on aspects of sociocultural theory in relation to second-language learning.

This page intentionally left blank

SECTION C

Teaching

This page intentionally left blank

Chapter 9

Methodologies

This chapter examines methodology in ESP and describes four macrostrategies used in teaching. The term *macrostrategy* was coined by Stern (1992) to refer to an overriding methodological principle covering a wide variety of classroom techniques and procedures at the planned level of teaching. The chapter illustrates strategies found in ESP teaching, using instructional materials and lesson plans developed by teachers for specific classes. Some of the materials have subsequently been published. Instructional materials and lesson plans embody views of learning (Tomlinson, 1998). These views of learning can be inferred from the activities the materials and plans propose and how they are sequenced. For example, three different teachers of English for Business Purposes develop instructional materials with a common focus—a role play about dealing with difficult customers in a service encounter. The material developed by one teacher incorporates a 'language focus' stage (ways to express acknowledgement) prior to a role-play task. The material developed by the second teacher does not include a language focus stage at all, and that of the third teacher does include a language focus stage (again, ways to express acknowledgment) but sequenced after the role-play stage and in the form of a debriefing. The material of the first teacher incorporated a language description stage before a student production stage (the role play). It may be inferred from this that the teacher expects that drawing the students' attention to language forms prior to production work may result in the students using those forms in their production. The teacher sees these stages and sequencing as beneficial for learning. The material of the second teacher involves a student production task (the role play) only. The material of the third teacher includes a language description stage but it is sequenced after the role play. The teacher may expect that when students have first struggled to produce their own language in the role play they will be mentally receptive to a description of language that highlights language they needed but lacked for the role play. In this chapter I link ideas in the literature on second language acquisition to materials developed by ESP teachers. The links I describe are based on inferences I have made.

It has been noted that ESP teachers tend to produce their own instructional materials rather than relying on commercially produced ones (Hutchinson & Waters, 1987). This can be attributed largely to the fact that ESP classes are convened to deal with the specific needs of the students. Such needs can usually be addressed only partially by commercially available materials that were developed with a general audience in mind. Examination of the instructional materials and plans can offer insights into the 'practical consciousness' (see discussion of *Structuration Theory* in chapter 2) of ESP teachers.

It is debatable whether ESP has a distinctive methodology. Robinson (1991) argues that methodology in English Language Teaching (ELT) and ESP differ little and that it is not possible to say whether general ELT has borrowed ideas for methodology from ESP or whether ESP has borrowed ideas from general ELT. Robinson identifies two characteristic features of ESP methodology: ESP can base activities on students' specialism (but need not do so), and ESP activities can (but may not) have a truly authentic purpose derived from students' target needs. Dudley-Evans and St. John (1998) maintain that what characterizes ESP methodology is the use of tasks and activities reflecting the students' specialist areas. Postexperience ESP learners have specialist knowledge from working or studying in their specialist areas and a 'deep-end strategy' (p. 190) can be used. In a deep-end strategy, students' performance of a task is the point of departure for instruction. Watson Todd (2003) reports that six approaches have been emphasised in the EAP literature: inductive learning, process syllabuses, learner autonomy, use of authentic materials and tasks, integration of teaching and technology and team teaching (cooperating with content teachers). Watson Todd argues that whereas the first five are also found in general English language teaching, the sixth, team teaching or cooperation with content teachers, is distinctive to EAP.

The discussion of methodologies presented in the chapter is organized around the concepts of input and output. These concepts are associated with information processing views of second language acquisition as discussed in chapter 8. They will be familiar to most language teachers, and for this reason, I have chosen them as a means of organizing the discussion.

INPUT-BASED STRATEGIES

Input based strategies rest on the idea that learning occurs primarily through exposure to language input in the form of written or spoken texts and language descriptions. Input is seen as a sine qua non of learning. Two distinct subcategories of input-based strategies can be identified. The first is premised on the idea that input is sufficient for learning and the second on the idea that input needs to be followed by student output for learning to occur.

Predominantly Input

Concepts

In this strategy, students are primarily provided with language input inasmuch as exposure to it is understood to promote learning. Learning comes about as the students see evidence (sometimes also termed *positive evidence*) of how language works or how language is used in workplace, academic, or professional target environments. Students do not need to be pushed into immediate production in order to learn.

The input strategy can be linked to ideas of language learning proposed by Krashen (1982), who argued that learners develop their linguistic abilities in the absence of explicit instruction. Explicit instruction about language and conscious study of language lead only to 'learning.' Learnt knowledge functions as a monitor—learners use it to monitor their production of language. The ability to produce language, however, derives from acquisition—unconscious and gradual development of language through exposure to comprehensible input.

Teaching can simply provide positive evidence about how language works or is used by exposing students to authentic texts and engaging them in comprehension activities. Or teaching can go beyond this simple exposure to language input and aim to help students notice specific language features or forms in it through the use of awareness-raising activities (alternatively termed *consciousness-raising* activities). Through the use of such activities, teachers aim to direct students' attention to the targeted forms or features in the input so that the students will develop explicit knowledge of them. There are a number of techniques for awareness raising, such as input flooding (exposure to multiple samples of the feature) and input enhancement (the feature is highlighted in the text).

Heightened awareness of the forms or features by the students is understood to be beneficial. It is not expected that once students have become aware of a linguistic item, they will immediately produce it, but rather that repeated noticing will enhance learning. Acquisition, argues Tomlinson (1998) 'results from the gradual and dynamic process of internal generalization rather than from instant adjustments to the learner's internal grammar' (p. 16). It is important for learners to be reexposed to language items in multiple samples over time. The use of reading and listening texts are one way to achieve this. There can be a gap between learners' understanding or becoming aware of a linguistic item and actually activating this knowledge into some form of production.

Research

Classroom-based second language acquisition research has shown that learners can acquire some linguistic features 'incidentally'—thus showing that instruction does not need to target these features as they can be learnt from input in the environment (Lightbrown, 2000). Although it is now generally agreed that learners do acquire language that was not the focus of explicit teaching, there is less consensus about the extent to which this is an unconscious process as originally hypothesized by Krashen (1982). Research has shown that exposure to comprehensible input alone does not lead to all types of learning equally. It is more likely to lead to the development of communicativeness and fluency than to gains in linguistic accuracy (Ellis, Basturkmen, & Loewen, 2001).

Erlam (2003) reviews research studies that contrasted the effectiveness of structured input-based instruction with output-based instruction. Structured input-based instruction was defined as instruction in which students work with language input in the form of listening and reading tasks. The tasks focus the students' attention on a specific target form. The students are required to notice the form and process its meaning. All the studies reviewed showed that students who had received structured input-based instruction performed as well on tests of comprehension and interpretation as students who had received output-based instruction. More surprisingly, a number of studies reviewed reported equivalent gains on tests of production for students who had received structured input-based instruction and those who had received output-based instruction.

Applications

The following examples can be linked to input-based teaching. The first example illustrates a teaching strategy based on the idea of implicit knowledge acquisition through exposure alone and the second illustrates consciousness-raising activities.

Example 1: Subject Specialist Texts for Comprehension. The ESP division of the English Language Centre at Cukurova University, Turkey provides English language instruction for students in their first and second years of study in their departments in the university. The ESP courses focus on the vocabulary of the students' disciplines and how concepts and ideas are expressed in them.

One commonly adopted lesson plan employed at the Centre involves the use of subject specialist texts for comprehension activities. An authentic text is chosen on the basis of topic and level. The topic of the text needs to be relevant to learners' specialist interests. For example, one ESP instructor chose a text on the subject of religious festivals in different counties for her ESP class composed of students studying theology. The text also needs to be slightly above the students' current level of comprehension. It should contain some but not too many structures and vocabulary items that are not well known to the students.

The text is given out for self-study in the first instance. Students read the text and isolate the vocabulary items in the text that they do not know and translate them into their first language.

In class the teacher leads a discussion (this is done in Turkish, which is the first language of the teacher and students) on the meaning of segments of the text the teacher preselects as 'interesting' from a content point of view. During the discussions, the teacher periodically draws students' attention to linguistic features of the input arising incidentally when engaged in the discussion of meaning of the text.

Example 2: Awareness-Raising Activities. To illustrate awareness-raising activities, I have chosen two lesson plans for EAP classes from a published collection of teaching ideas (Master & Brinton, 1998). In both cases, the lessons try to help students develop their ability to notice and become more aware of language use and communication in their disciplines.

Listen Up (shown in Fig. 9.1) involves students observing and reflecting on in situ university lectures. The aim is to raise students' awareness of aspects of nonverbal communication used in lectures. Instruction involves using prerecorded videos of lectures and also getting students to go out into the university environment.

Genre Files (shown in Fig. 9.2) involves students collecting documents from their target environments and drawing students' attention to genre-related features in the input.

Input to Output

Concepts

In this strategy, students are provided with input as the basis for production (output). The lack of sufficient use of this strategy can be inferred in the following criticism made of methodology in ESP: 'A common failing in teaching is to expect high level production without giving sufficient input' (Scott & Scott, 1984, p. 217).

In instruction based on this strategy, the focus is on students acquiring explicit knowledge of preselected language items. The teacher selects specific items (target linguistic forms or features) as the focus of instruction. The items are presented or highlighted by the teacher. This is followed by

Listen Up!

Levels
Intermediate +

Aims
Comprehend lectures
Recognize and identify
nonverbal patterns in
U.S. discourse

Class Time
50 minutes
(presentation)
50 minutes (discussion)

Preparation Time
Variable

Resources
Videotaped lectures or
slides of professors in
various lecture poses
Notes on nonverbal
communication in U.S.
discourse

This activity helps the students comprehend academic lectures by recognizing and looking for nonverbal patterns in U.S. discourse. After the teacher discusses and demonstrates the gestures faculty use when lecturing, the students apply the concepts to slides or videos of faculty (ideally from their current courses) and to nonverbal language in their own culture.

Procedure

1. Have the students arrange their chairs in a large semicircle so they can see each other. Model the gestures used for emphasis in lectures in three categories: (a) arms and hands, (b) legs and posture, and (c) head and face (see the Appendix).
2. Have the students discuss how their current content instructors use nonverbal language to emphasize the main ideas in a lecture.
3. Show slides of professors giving lectures, and have the students comment on the gestures. Alternatively, play a segment from a videotaped lecture, and have the students analyze and comment on the gestures.
4. Have the students discuss nonverbal communication practices in their own cultures, noting differences and similarities.
5. Ask the students to attend a lecture, take notes, analyze the lecture for nonverbal emphasis of main ideas, and write a five-paragraph essay summarizing their findings. In the essay, have them discuss the strengths and limitations of their lecture notes, identify the organizational pattern of the lecturer, and analyze the lecturer's nonverbal communication behaviors, voice clues, and transition-word clues.
6. In the following class, have the students share their findings in groups of four. Rotate the students from one group to another until all the students have had a chance to listen to everyone's observations.

Appendix: Emphasis Gestures for Lectures

Category	Gesture
Arms and hands	Steepling
	Open hands
	Pointing
	Writing on the blackboard
	Gripping the podium
	Using the fingers to count out points or ideas
	Clenching the fist
	Using an extension such as chalk, a coffee cup, a ruler, or glasses
	Rubbing palms together
	Rubbing chalk between palms
	Moving hands and arms forward from body
Legs and posture	Walking closer to the audience
	Pacing back and forth with deliberate strides
Head and face	Nodding
	Smiling

FIG. 9.1.   Sample material: Listen Up! From Starks-Martin, 1998 (pp. 103–105). Reprinted by permission.

some form of practice activity in which the students produce the items. The input can take various forms such as a language description, analysis of a genre, or teacher-led discussion of features in a text. The input provides accurate samples of how the language works and how it is used. The students become aware of a gap between how they currently understand or use the linguistic form or feature and the equivalent feature in target language use. The teacher then requires the students to produce (output) the targeted item(s), generally within the same lesson or the following lesson.

Research

White (1998) studied the acquisition of possessive determiners 'his' and 'her' with Francophone learners. The acquisition of this language feature is known to be problematic because of differences between the English and French rules for establishing the gender of third person singular (in French, Robert voit *sa* mere, but in English, Robert sees *his* mother; pp. 86–87). White found that the learners who were exposed to 'enhanced' input (multiple samples of the targeted items that had been highlighted in text-based input through bolding, underlining, or enlarging) were better able to use them in oral production tasks than those who had not received this enhanced input. Further experimental research by White, reported in Lightbrown (2000), involved instruction that provided learners with explicit information about the relationship between the possessive pronouns and the nouns to which they attached. White found that the students who had been provided with this type of instruction were able to use the possessive determiners in more advanced ways in an oral production task than those who had not.

Some research evidence supports the teaching of explicit knowledge about genres as input for production work. Henry and Roseberry (1998) report a study in which two groups of students were given classroom instruction using the same set of authentic texts. Students in Group A were given explicit, form-focused instruction analyzing the organization of moves in the genre of the tourist information texts. Instruction for students in Group B involved reading the texts and meaning-focused activities (cloze exercises and sentence joining). Following the instruction, the students were required to produce their own tourist information texts. Results showed that students in Group A outperformed students in Group B on two measures of success: ability to sequence information and ability to produce cohesive text. Students in Group A were also reported to have higher levels of motivation toward the instruction than students in Group B.

Loewen and Basturkmen (2005) investigated whether students made use of the genre-related information presented and highlighted in instruction in EAP writing instruction when they were later required to work in small groups to coconstruct a sample text. In the first phase of instruction,

Creating Lifetime Genre Files

Levels
Intermediate +

Aims
Become familiar with
written English genres

Class Time
20–30 minutes (initial
presentation)
Ongoing

Preparation Time
1 hour

Resources
Large, ringed notebooks
Blank genre profile
sheets
Completed genre profile
sheet

This lesson is designed to serve as one of the primary activities in an ES
writing course or to serve as a supplement to ESP reading, vocabular
or grammar instruction. The activity, which entails both independent an
instructor-guided learning, provides learners with a useful resource th:
they can continually use and expand throughout their careers.

Procedure

1. Explain the concept of genres, and show a few diverse examples (e.g.,
   journal article, wedding invitation, grant proposal, poem, insurance
   policy, letter of resignation, invoice, résumé, obituary).
2. Discuss and list some of the English genres that your students are
   likely to use during their lives. Mark those requiring immediate
   instructional attention with an asterisk.
3. Ask the students to begin collecting samples of these written English
   genres and putting them in a large, ringed notebook for ease of
   reference. If you wish, point the students to various World Wide Web
   sites, publications, or other sources to ease the search process. If the
   students have similar learning needs, have them work together.
4. Distribute copies of the genre profile sheet (see the Appendix), and
   ask the students to fill out one sheet to accompany each genre sample
   they obtain. Hand out a completed genre profile sheet for one of the
   genres shown in Step 1.
5. As the students assemble their individualized collections of English
   genre samples, draw on the material from time to time during the
   language course for studies of genre and the contextual, organizational, grammatical, and lexical features that distinguish each type.
   Studies might include creative analysis and imitation exercises as well
   as discussions of observed communication differences between
   members of various discourse communities. Be sure to add your input
   on the construction of accurate genre profiles.
6. Ask the students to continue adding genre samples to their personal
   collections after they complete their English program to encourage
   self-learning and to build a useful reference for future writing needs.
   Also have the students include samples of their own work, such as
   marked drafts and final products, to aid their learning.

FIG. 9.2. Sample material: Genre files. From Orr, 1998 (pp. 87–90).
Reprinted by permission.

the teacher focused the students' attention on features and forms typically
used in writing a data commentary text. In the following phase of instruction a week later, the students, working in groups of three, were required
to write a data commentary text to support a chart and numerical data
about rent increases in a particular country. The researchers recorded the
discussions between the students working on the group task and identified
the episodes during the interaction in which students discussed specific
linguistic forms and features. The study showed that the students engaged
in more episodes focused on genre-related topics than on other linguistic

Appendix:
Genre Profile
Sheet
	Genre: *Résumé*
	
	Purpose(s): *To market a person's education, work experience, and accomplishments in a persuasive manner to obtain a job interview.*
	
	Audience(s): *Person(s) responsible for personnel decisions (e.g., director of human resources)*
	
	Notes on content and format:
	
	1. *Name and contact information is centered at the top of the page or placed in the upper left margin. The font size is usually larger than that in the body of the document and frequently appears in boldface.*
	2. *Education, work experience, achievements, and other material appropriate for the intended reader are usually listed in descending chronological order under these or similar headings. The headings are usually in boldface and placed at the left margin with extra space above and below the heading.*
	3. *The document frequently ends with the heading "References" and the line "Available on request."*
	
	Notes on grammar and vocabulary:
	
	1. *The grammatical subject plus the auxiliary or linking verb is usually dropped in most statements related to work experience or accomplishments as in the following:*
	  ● *Recipient of the XXX Award for . . .*
	  ● *Awarded the YYY Prize for . . .*
	  ● *Designed software that . . .*
	  ● *Developed a training program for . . .*
	
	2. *Other options for "Available on request:"*
	  ● *Furnished on request.*
	  ● *Furnished upon request.*

FIG. 9.2 *(continued)*

topics such as grammar, vocabulary, and features of written text in general. The findings indicated that the students were able to make use of the type of linguistic information that had been presented to them by the teacher, in the first stage of instruction, in the production task in the second stage.

Applications

In ESP, the input-to-output option is used for teaching different aspects of language, including genre knowledge. Badger and White (2000) describe the practice of understanding (input) and applying rules (output) in the practice of genre instruction in ESP: 'Proponents of genre approaches are not often explicit about their theory of learning. However, the use of model texts and the idea of analysis suggest that learning is partly a question of imitation and partly a matter of understanding and consciously applying rules' (p. 156).

A number of criticisms have been made of the use of this option for teaching genres. This option is often referred to as a 'product approach' to teaching writing (Badger & White, 2000). Sengupta, Forey, and Hamp-Lyons (1999) criticize instruction of genres based on a 'show and tell approach' and that leads to a prescription for how to do a genre. Berkenkotter and Huckin (1993) argue that genre knowledge cannot be taught. It can only be acquired as people become enculturated into specific disciplines.

The input-to-output strategy can be inferred from the following pieces of instructional material. The first is a proposal for genre-based instruction for an English for Engineering studies class and the second is for teaching general English for Academic Purposes vocabulary.

Example 1: The Final Year Engineering Report. L. Flowerdew (2000, 2001) reports on the method used to teach students who were writing final-year engineering reports in a Hong Kong university. Flowerdew developed the materials in line with the recommendations of Hopkins and Dudley-Evans (1988), Kusel (1992), Dudley-Evans (1994), and Jacoby, Leech, and Holton (1995). The first step in developing the materials was to collect a small corpus of successful final year reports from former students. The reports were analysed for move sequence, use of graphics and visuals, and to identify the relationship between sections (for example, the relationship between the introduction and the results section).

The following stages and activities were used in teaching. The move sequence of the report was highlighted. Linguistic phrases used in the corpus were highlighted with the aim of expanding the students' own repertoire of ways to express engineering concepts. A text was cut into sections and the students reconstructed it. Sample texts were compared. The content of moves and sections was highlighted. 'Good models' of students' writing were provided by the engineering faculty and these were discussed in the EAP class. L. Flowerdew (2000) argues that good apprentice models offer 'realistic, attainable models of academic writing' (p. 369).

Example 2: Academic Vocabulary. Thursten and Candlin (1998) offer a proposal for teaching general academic vocabulary. Instruction is based on the use of concordances (see Fig. 9.3). The concordances involve vocabulary items that research had shown to occur frequently in a corpus of academic writing. Each lesson focuses on a set of vocabulary items. Concordances of these items are used as the input in instruction. The concordances are used in the following ways:

1. Students are presented with a concordance (multiple examples of a vocabulary item used in context). Instruction leads the students to 'notice' how the word is used.

```
UNIT 5A
LOOK
Study these concordances, underlining the central group of words which can stand
alone, as has been done in the first example. Then answer the questions below. You
may like to look at question 1 before you start. (Don't worry that these are cut-off
sentences - just familiarize yourself with the key words).

GROUP 1
e seen at puberty. The isolation and chemical identification of several sex hormones in the late 192
akhtin's method lies not simply in the formal identification of a genre or a subgenre or a chronotop
 established only after much controversy. Its identification was an early success of X-ray crystallo
o the production of muscle-specific proteins. Identification of the new muscle proteins was made pos
loration of their difficulties had led to the identification of two additional problems: <list> <ite
GROUP 2
ure of construction as a whole; the facts are identified by the principles that result.          In
erapy, and that such attitudes can usually be identified by carefully analysing the patient's attemp
 occurrence of a linguistic form which can be identified as Arabic. Christianity had a similar cohes
existence. <p> Another of many criteria to be identified could be the subsequent or continuing costs
2 BC), who rejected the idea that time can be identified with any form of motion or change. For, he
l Greek literature, can nevertheless still be identified as a distinctive and possibly definitive ge
operties. <p> Many more carcinogens have been identified since then. Some are mainly of laboratory i
runs of mutual recrimination. <p> So, we have identified two characteristics of winning strategies:
ver the last three hundred years or so. It is identified by a series of political causes espoused by
orerunners of Islam. A later Muslim tradition identified the Rock as the point from which Muhammad a
ed by Levene's tetra-structure. The sugar was identified as either ribose or deoxyribose: for a time
random). Forty years later these factors were identified as bits of chromosome, and a century later
er supply 20 years or so before bacteria were identified as causing the disease. Lime juice was reco
 Up to five stages in the life cycle could be identified, each of which might respond to a different
r estimated eight hundred buildings have been identified. Her techniques and their results were by n
GROUP 3
ey do not rejoin. If we knew enough and could identify all the individual animals alive, say, one hu
st, policies must be changed. <p> We can only identify the proper criteria correctly if we accept th
 the therapist's role is to help the partners identify the problems that they face as a couple and t
ood is out of bounds in politics. It tries to identify the reasons which lead people to embrace this
hough less widely researched. Here, I want to identify one feature of that relationship which seems
r separate effects. Research was essential to identify the ill-effects attributable to each substanc
tion relative to that tradition. They hope to identify a coherent body of ideas which places them so
ndon School of Hygiene, where he continued to identify the chemical constituents of fungi and discov
```

```
FAMILIARIZE
1) Which of the following statements do you think are true? Tick your
answer in the box.

TO IDENTIFY involves naming                             true ☐        false ☐
TO IDENTIFY involves describing                         true ☐        false ☐
TO IDENTIFY involves imagining                          true ☐        false ☐
TO IDENTIFY involves deciding what something is         true ☐        false ☐
TO IDENTIFY involves recognizing                        true ☐        false ☐
TO IDENTIFY involves criticizing                        true ☐        false ☐
```

FIG. 9.3.   Concordance on "identity." Reprinted from *English for Specific Purposes*, Vol. 17, J. Thurstun and C. N. Candlin, "Concordancing and the teaching . . ." (p. 272). Copyright © 1998, with permission from Elsevier Science.

2. Students answer questions on the meaning and use of the items based on their examination of the concordance input. For example, one exercise requires students to notice the kind of objects that are 'identified.'

3. Controlled practice and freer practice activities are provided so that the students use the item in written production.

OUTPUT-BASED STRATEGIES

Output-based instruction takes as its starting point students' efforts to communicate in the target language. Two substrategies can be identified. The first is based on the premise that using the language (producing output) is sufficient for learning and the second on the premise that it is only when students' production or output is followed by some form of input (discussion or highlighting of language) that learning occurs.

Predominantly Output

Concepts

In instruction based on a predominantly output strategy, students are placed in situations that require them to perform production tasks (to produce output) at the outset of a lesson or activity. The rationale is that through producing language, students can identify where their interlanguage (developing language system) is sufficient for the performance or production task and where it is not. Swain (1985, 1998) argues that in being pushed to produce, language learners notice 'holes' in their linguistic repertoire and this stimulates learning of language to fill in the holes. Thus it is through being required to use language that one's language develops because while endeavouring to communicate through the language learners become aware of missing elements in their linguistic repertoire. This is termed the *the output hypothesis.*

Ellis (1990, p. 117) identifies three key points in Swain's argument for the role of output in advancing levels of grammatical language accuracy:

• The need to produce output ('pushed language use') that is precise, coherent, and appropriate during negotiation of meaning encourages the learners to develop the necessary grammatical resources.

• During output, the learners can try out their hypotheses about language. Production, as opposed to comprehension, may force the learner to move from semantic to syntactic processing. It is possible to comprehend a message without any syntactic analysis of the input it contains.

• Production is the trigger that forces learners to pay attention to the means of expression.

Research

Investigations of students in French immersion classes in Canada revealed that they often failed to develop their grammatical and sociolinguistic accuracy despite many years of plentiful exposure to input. Swain (1985) argued that this failure was due to the fact that the students had received few opportunities to produce language. Most of the interaction in the classes had been teacher-led. Swain proposed that in addition to comprehensible input, learners need to be pushed to use their language in communicative situations. Teaching needs to provide learners with opportunities to use whatever linguistic resources they have at their disposal.

A key idea in the output hypothesis is that learners develop a second language when pushed to do so. Research provides some evidence for this theory. Pica's (1988) study, reported in Ellis (1990), showed that learners' output became more grammatically accurate following exchanges in which their interlocutor requested clarification from them compared to exchanges in which the interlocutor simply requested confirmation. Having to clarify what has been said calls for careful consideration of how to express and encode a message. In a confirmation request, it is the interlocutor who must consider and work out how to express the message or encode the idea. In other words, the interaction showed that when the learners were pushed into output by clarification requests, they improved their grammatical accuracy.

Not all production tasks, however, lead to the type of the interaction needed for negotiation of meaning and pushed output. Seedhouse (1999) examined the interaction of students working on convergent tasks (tasks where students come together to agree on something) and found that the students often made little use of explicit language and relied on minimal responses and contributions because they had shared reference systems. The tasks had not pushed the students to call on the range of linguistic resources they had.

Applications

The idea of students being required to produce language is reflected in many task-based activities for the classroom. In line with Willis (1990), a task is understood to be 'an activity that involves the use of language but in which the focus is on the outcome of the activity rather than on the language used to achieve that outcome' (p. 127). Tasks specify what students will communicate about and action they will take but do not specify the language that students will use or are expected to learn in the process of doing the task (Ellis, 1998). Such activities do not set out to teach a preselection of linguistic items as it is recognised that any preselection of language items to be taught is unlikely to match the learner's internal syllabus. It is claimed that tasks create the conditions for acquisition, such as negotiation of meaning, and that doing tasks enables learners to develop the language and skills in line with their own internal syllabuses (Ellis, 1998).

Task-based teaching has featured strongly in ESP in recent years and is used often in combination with a 'deep-end strategy'—student performance as the point of departure for the lesson and for which students may or may not have been given preparation time (Dudley-Evans & St. John, 1998). Dudley Evans and St. John argue that a benefit of the strategy is that it reflects the students' target or professional, academic, or workplace world where performance is the point of departure rather than preparation. In ESP the use of deep-end strategy is associated with case study activities, projects, presentations, role plays, and simulations.

Two teaching activities are given next to illustrate the output option. The first is a project (written production) and the second is a simulation (spoken production).

Example 1: E-Commerce Web Page Project. Crookes (2001) reports a project used for teaching English for Business Purposes in Australia. The project calls for the students to set up an e-commerce web page for small businesses in the local community. The students carry out this project during the final weeks of the program. The students are young adults with good computer skills.

The project involved the following steps:

- The class examined commercial Internet sites.
- Students discussed web page design techniques in class.
- The task was given. The task was to advertise a local business with a 3-page linked Web site.
- Out-of-class pairs of students met with a local business owner to find out the goods/services the business owner would like advertised on the web.
- Back in the ESP class, the pairs prepared the Web-site advertisement.

In this task the students were required to create an advertisement that accurately conveyed information about the business (pushed output). The output emerged during a process of negotiation of meaning—first in terms of negotiated content with the business owners and second as the pairs negotiated the language needed to convey the information about the business.

Example 2: Workplace Project Team Meeting Simulation. This task involves a simulation of a workplace meeting (see Fig. 9.4). The students are required to find a solution to a problem and present the solution in the form of a flowchart. There is no preselected linguistic input, and students can make use of any linguistic resources they have at their disposal. The impetus for pushed output comes in Steps 9 and 10. Both steps push students to report accurately on concepts and ideas. Step 10 requires students to make clarifications (a force for pushed input suggested by the research findings of Pica, 1988).

Output to Input

Concepts

In instruction based on an output-to-input strategy, students' production (output) is followed by feedback. Students perform a task and feedback is provided to show a more native-like performance. The aim is that the students notice how their own output differs from the more native-like model. The feedback stage may be followed by a further optional stage in which students reperform the task.

During task production, students notice 'holes' in their linguistic repertoire or resources, thus creating the metacognitive state necessary for input. Learners may notice that they cannot say what they want to say precisely in the target language—'noticing a hole in one's inter-language' (Swain, 1998, p. 66). It is thought that provision of input in advance of students' themselves recognizing a need for it is similar to expecting someone to be interested in filling a crack in the plaster work on the wall before they have perceived that there is a gap to be filled.

This strategy does not involve a focus on prespecified linguistic items. No particular language forms are targeted for instruction, although a general area may be (for example, how to make requests, doing a business proposal). Feedback may be given on any number of language items. Teachers may collect examples of errors or interesting aspects of language use that arose during the production stage. These are to give feedback to the whole class or to individual students, pairs, and groups.

In an output-to-input strategy, the learning activity or task functions to create the conditions for students to 'notice a hole' in their linguistic repertoire and produce 'data' for feedback. Activities in the input stage provide opportunities for students to notice the gap by comparing their output with more native-like performance. Once they have noticed the gap, they are psychologically ready for information provided in feedback (the input stage) because they have experienced difficulty, recognized a hole in their linguistic repertoire, and thus have sharpened attention to the input provided.

Applications

The output–input option is illustrated with reference to two pieces of teaching material for teaching academic speaking.

Example 1: Promoting Pragmatic Awareness and Spoken Discourse With EAP Classes by Clennell (1999). The material focuses on understanding and interpreting spoken discourse. The following teaching procedure was used: The first stage requires students to produce output. Students working in pairs choose a topic and develop an interview protocol to use to interview native speakers on the campus. They conduct and record a number of interviews. The students transcribe one of the interviews and present their transcription and analysis of events in it to the class.

The second stage provides opportunities for input or feedback to students on their performance of the task. To present their work, the pairs

Minds Meeting

Levels
Advanced

Aims
Work in teams with a
specific agenda
Express a plan as a
flowchart
Write minutes of
meetings

Class Time
1 hour

Preparation Time
30-60 minutes

Resources
Task sheet
Agenda sheet
Meeting agenda handout
Overhead projector,
transparencies, and pens

This activity simulates a workplace project team meeting. It closely integrates several language activities: practicing with professional workplace procedures, using language for planning and decision making, and recording oral interactions in both diagrammatic and written forms. Because the students are expected to produce a flowchart to demonstrate the coordination of a project, the verbal interaction is engaging and purposeful. The homework exercise of writing up the minutes, in which accuracy of form and content are important, is also experience based.

Procedure

1. Devise a task sheet outlining a problem, the solution of which can be addressed by groups and then recorded as flowcharts. Alternatively, use the task in the Appendix.
2. Explain to the students that they will be taking part in a workplace simulation. In a meeting, they will plan a project, a secretary will take minutes, and they will record their plan as a flowchart. The team leader of each group will present these results on an overhead transparency (OHT).
3. Divide the class into teams of four or five students, preferably at tables.
4. Choose team leaders and give them each an OHT and a pen.
5. Give each team member a copy of the task sheet and an agenda sheet.
6. Instruct the teams to select a secretary to take notes and a scribe to draft the flowchart.
7. Direct the teams to spend 20-25 minutes discussing the plan in response to the task sheet and drafting the flowchart, making it as realistic as they can, while the secretary takes minutes.

FIG. 9.4.   Sample material: Minds meeting. From Clerehan and Croslin, 1998 (pp. 239–241). Reprinted by permission.

replay the recording and talk through their transcription and analysis of events. Peers and the teacher offer suggestions and can disagree with the deciphering and the analysis of events as presented. In Clennell's class, students in the audience point out language items and features that eluded or confused the interviewers. For example, one pair of students transcribed, 'It's pretty shocking what happen er I mean. . . .' Students in the audience identified what was actually said as, 'It's pretty shocking what happened there, I mean . . .'

Example 2: Discourse in Seminars and Questions.   In this material the production (output) stage requires students to predict and write down questions they would be asked following a presentation. They are also required

<table>
<tr><td></td><td>

8. Direct each team to draw its flowchart on an OHT.
9. Ask each team leader to present the team's flowchart, briefly justifying the team's decisions.
10. Direct each team to look at the secretary's notes and clarify anything that is not clear, as each team member will need to write up the minutes of the meeting.
11. Photocopy each team's notes, and give the copies to team members.
12. Assign the writing up of the minutes as homework.

</td></tr>
</table>

Caveats and Options

1. The activity is most successful with a class that has a professional orientation. It was devised for engineering students but can be used with students of business, computing, and the like.
2. Precede the activity by a session in which you discuss the purpose and practice of taking and writing up minutes, preferably providing a sample or two. If not, do so at the beginning of class.
3. For Step 7, put the task sheet on an OHT to keep all the students focused.
4. Depending on the students' language and interest levels, encourage them to make the flowcharts as detailed as they want, imagining the processes in time and space. If you wish, introduce an element of competitiveness, again depending on the overall class dynamics and your objectives.
5. Note that the team leader's presentation need only be short.
6. Either assess the minutes yourself, or have the students do so.

Appendix: Task and Agenda

> Task: You are the manufacturing manager of a company that makes office equipment. Your market research shows that there is a demand for the development of a new product: an automatic envelope sealer. You are meeting with a small, executive project team to plan the project. The group is aiming to coordinate the activities of the following departments: design, sales, production, packaging, warehouse, and delivery. These departments need to know what they have to do and which other departments they need to cooperate with. Your group must
> - appoint a secretary to take minutes (All the students will be given a photocopy of the minutes at the end of the lesson.)
> - conduct the meeting in accordance with the agenda
> - draw up a flowchart to show the desired progression of events and the coordination of the departments
>
> You will be required to write up the minutes from the photocopy for homework.

> Austral Office Equipment
> Project Team Meeting
> Agenda
>
> 1. Business arising
>
>   1.1 New product
>
> 2. Manufacturing plan and responsibilities of departments
>
> 3. Development of flowchart
>
> 4. Other business

FIG. 9.4 *(continued)*

Sample material of a task-based activity

Student A

Stage One: Explanation of aims

By the end of the session you will have learnt about some of the ways people make "difficult questions" and presenters deal with them after a presentation. You will also have practised formulating responses to "difficult questions".

Stage Two: Task Preparation

You are going to present a three minute presentation and deal with some questions from the audience after it.

The Moritsu company is currently deciding whether to produce the G4X or G2X engine. Your group will read the notes provided on both products and company background and prepare a case presentation in which your group explains why your company should produce G4X. Read the case study notes provided.

Note down your arguments for this product and plan your presentation briefly.

Stage Three: Language focus

Some members of the audience will question your decision to produce the G4X. In your group predict what arguments they may make. Write down two of the questions they may ask. How would you respond? Make notes in your group.

Consult the two text samples, A and B, of questions and responses.

1. What is similar in the student questions in samples A and B?
2. Do the presenters in samples A & B accept the audience members' criticisms? How do they respond to these criticisms?
— How does A structure his response and how does B?
3. What strategies does presenter A choose and why?
4. Can you think of any other ways that A and B might formulate their responses?

Stage Four: Application

1. Now you have seen how a speaker dealt with a difficult question. Go back to the difficult questions you predict that you may be asked about your choice of product G4X and plan how you would respond.
2. Give your presentation on your choice of G4X to the other group. Afterwards take questions. The interaction will be recorded.

Stage Five: Evaluation

1. Listen to the recording. Can you identify the difficult questions? What

were they? How did you deal with them? How did you formulate your responses and why?
2. If you were to respond to those question again, what, if anything, would you do differently?
3. Write down the questions and your responses on a OHT and explain to the class how they were formulated and what strategies you used. Explain any alternatives you think might have been better.

Stage Six: Discussion on discourse and culture

1. Would the interaction have been different in your country?
2. What kinds of strategies do you have in your culture for making and dealing with "difficult questions" in this kind of event?

Sample A

S I think one point I know it's rare for you to have the pleasure of hearing my voice but nevertheless one point I think needs raising. You mentioned one of the strengths of both these companies was its chief executive directors. By the very nature of them being the main individuals concerned with the success of these what happens when they reach the age of maturity and decide to leave or whatever. They might die or whatever happens I mean I would suggest that is a major weakness. That I would suggest is a major weakness.

P Well I mean in both cases they'd be replaced. And the evidence would suggest that there would still be Hanson there in the subsidiary. The guy is still very much in control. So I would suggest there is a risk but he's probably been well groomed and knows exactly what's required.

Sample B

S The previous group seem to have far more stress on the technology importance than yourselves. Didn't you feel that as a factor?

B I think I think it's irrelevant. You don't need it. You don't buy a TV on the basis of technology. I don't think you buy it on the technology. I think you need to keep up with it because if they get well down their competitors can use it against them. But I don't think it's important.

Notes:

1. A cassette recorder is needed for each group.
2. B students would argue the case for producing G2X.
3. Stage Six of this activity may be less important for some groups of learners, e.g. those who are studying English for university courses in their own countries.
4. Stage Two could begin by being teacher-led with teacher questions to check understanding of the task and comprehension of the written notes.

FIG. 9.5. Discourse in seminars and questions. Reprinted from *English for Specific Purposes*, Vol. 18, H. Basturkmen, "Discourse in MBA Seminars" (p. 73), Copyright © 1999, with permission from Elsevier Science.

to predict how they would respond to any difficult questions. Following this, students are provided with input (transcribed talk of seminar discussion), and they are led to notice how difficult questions were dealt with in the transcript. This provides an opportunity for the students to compare their own language production (their notes on language use) with a more native-like version. (See Fig. 9.5).

SUMMARY

The discussion of methodologies in ESP in this chapter was organized around four macrostrategies for teaching: predominantly input; input to output; predominantly output; and output to input. Two of these strategies were input-based. The first (predominantly input) was linked to the idea that learning occurs through students being exposed to samples of language use. The second (input to output) was linked to the idea that learners need first notice language forms and features and then use them in their own production. The teacher (or course designer) selects which items are to be presented for students to notice and thus learn.

Two output-based strategies were described. Predominantly output was linked to the idea that learning occurs through students struggling to communicate and being pushed to reach their linguistic ceilings. The output-to-input strategy was associated with the idea that learners are ready to acquire new language when they have experienced a hole (a lacuna) in their linguistic repertoire and are offered a solution to that problem in the form of feedback.

QUESTIONS FOR DISCUSSION AND PROJECTS

1. What role do the four macrostrategies described in this chapter play in your own teaching? Do you tend to use any of the strategies more than others?
2. Is a deep-end strategy suitable and desirable in the ESP class you currently teach or the type of class you are likely to teach in the future? Discuss the advantages and disadvantages of this strategy.
3. L. Flowerdew (2000, 2001) called on the engineering faculty at her university to provide samples of 'good' student writing that she used in teaching report writing. In teaching ESP or EAP, have you called on subject specialists to provide input for instruction or feedback on student production? If so, how?
4. What use of project work and case method studies do you make in your ESP teaching? In groups, draw up a list of the advantages and drawbacks

of these activities and discuss ways you would deal with any difficulties that may emerge.

5. In groups, discuss whether choice of teaching strategy is largely context-dependant or a matter of personal preference? Are teachers more likely to opt mainly for an output-based strategy because they have classes of mature and postexperienced ESP learners or because they espouse the concepts associated with output-based teaching?

FURTHER READING

- In the introduction to an edited volume on materials development in language teaching, Tomlinson (1998) discusses links between second language acquisition research and materials development.
- Watson Todd (2003) argues that the topic of methodology has been neglected in the literature on EAP and discusses whether EAP has a distinctive methodology.
- The introduction to Erlam's (2003) article offers a useful overview of the range of input- or output-based instructional activities.
- Ellis (2003) provides an in-depth examination of the relationship between task-based teaching and research on second language acquisition.
- Esteban and Canado (2004) review the use of case studies in ESP and identify some of the drawbacks associated with this technique. The writers show a practical example of using a case study in teaching English to postgraduate students of foreign trade and how they dealt with the difficulties involved.

Chapter 10

Objectives in Teaching ESP

This chapter examines broad objectives in teaching ESP. The chapter describes five objectives:

- To reveal subject-specific language use.
- To develop target performance competencies.
- To teach underlying knowledge.
- To develop strategic competence.
- To foster critical awareness.

The chapter also reviews the sociopolitical issues emerging in the ESP literature in recent years. Until recently, it had been commonly assumed that ESP teaching was a benign and neutral operation that simply set out to help nonnative speakers of English cope with language demands in their target environments. This assumption has now been questioned and calls have been made for a critical approach to ESP teaching.

In the chapter, reference is made to Stern's (1989, 1992) categorization of language education objectives. Stern distinguished four types of objectives: proficiency, knowledge, affective, and transfer. *Proficiency objectives* concern mastery of skills such as reading, writing, listening, and speaking. *Knowledge objectives* concern the acquisition of linguistic and cultural information. Linguistic knowledge objectives include language analysis and awareness of the systematic aspects of language. Cultural knowledge objectives include control of sociocultural rules (mastery of the norms of society, values, and orientations) and also the ability to recognise culturally significant facts, knowing what is acceptable and what is not. *Affective objectives* concern the development of positive feelings toward the subject of study. They include attitudes toward attaining second language competence, sociocultural competence, and language learning. *Transfer objectives* concern the ability to generalise from what has been learnt in one situation to other situations.

The following sections describe the five broad objectives in ESP teaching listed in the opening paragraph. Some ESP teachers reading this chapter will find that their teaching is oriented closely to one or two of the objectives described in the following pages. Others might find that all five objectives are important in their teaching. The organization of the sections differs slightly from that followed in previous chapters, with research and applications examined concurrently rather than consecutively.

TO REVEAL SUBJECT-SPECIFIC LANGUAGE USE

Concepts

Historically, the objective of teaching content about subject-specific language use has dominated ESP. This objective is linked to the linguistic knowledge objective and, to a lesser extent, the cultural knowledge objective in Stern's categorisation (1992). Teaching oriented to this objective aims to show how English is used in the target environment and to impart to students the knowledge about it that has been revealed by linguistic research in the field. There is a direct link between research and pedagogy, with teaching primarily focused on demonstrating the forms and features that descriptive linguistic research has brought to light.

Research and Applications

The idea that ESP teaching should be first and foremost concerned with demonstration of findings from linguistic research in specific-purpose language use can be seen in the recommendations made by Bhatia (1982). Bhatia made an in-depth linguistic analysis of the language of 'qualification' in legal texts. Following this, Bhatia offers a number of suggestions for teaching English to students of law. Teachers are advised to discuss the organization of texts with the students, to highlight the structure of the texts, and demonstrate the language of qualification in legal writing. Bhatia does not propose that research findings are simply presented in teaching, however. He recommends that teachers need to simplify example texts so that the structures used in legislative writing can be made more transparent to the learners.

The objective of revealing specific-purpose language use is intuitively appealing, but what might the potential drawbacks be of teaching and learning based on descriptions of specific-purpose language use? Wharton (1999) reviews research into the difficulties experienced in learning genres. Wharton's findings show that teaching and learning a genre involves far more than transmission of linguistic information. Her findings include the following points:

• Learners find academic and professional genre acquisition difficult because it necessitates not only development of conceptual understanding of the surface discourse but also of a set of socially valued norms and thus new frameworks of reasoning.
• Learning genres tends to be mastered late even in one's first language.
• It is difficult for teachers to communicate the nature of a genre to those who are unfamiliar with it.

Nearly two decades ago, in a discussion of teaching English for Science, Swales (1985) noted that ESP needed to go beyond simply revealing the truth about the language of science. He argued that ESP teaching needed to do more than 'simply import into the ESP classroom examples and practice work that reflected the grammatical, lexical, rhetorical and textual features of text types' (p. 174). The objectives described in the following sections represent four different orientations to teaching ESP, orientations that aim to do more than reveal subject-specific language use.

TO DEVELOP TARGET PERFORMANCE COMPETENCIES

Concepts

Competency-based occupational education can be described as an approach focused on developing the ability to perform the activities of an occupation and function to the standards expected of those employed in that occupation (Funnel & Owen, 1992). In language education, teaching oriented toward this objective presents language operationally in terms of what people do with language and the skills they need to do it. Courses are organized around core skills and competencies that are also subdivided into microskills and more specific competencies. This orientation can be categorized as a proficiency objective, according to Stern's classification (1992).

The link between needs analysis and teaching to develop target performance competencies is straightforward. Needs analysis reveals the demands and expectations of the target environment, and ESP teaching sets out to help students meet those demands to the level of competency expected. For example, a hypothetical needs analysis reveals that one of the competencies needed by medical practitioners is the ability to ask questions to elicit personal medical histories from patients. An ESP course devised for overseas-trained doctors might specify this competency as a course objective: 'by the end of the course students should be able to ask questions in English to elicit medical histories in clinical settings.'

One early proposal for ESP teaching oriented directly toward the demands of the target environment was the Communicative Needs Processor proposed by Munby (1978). Munby suggested that courses could be developed around the communicative events in which ESP students would be engaged in their target environment. Needs analysis was used to identify communicative events occurring routinely in the target workplace and the speech acts they involved. A list of language exponents and formulaic expressions for the speech acts was created. The inventory of communicative events, speech acts, and language exponents became a specification for ESP course content. One drawback of this proposal was that it failed to take into account the fact that encounters in real life situations are often unpredictable and events develop in surprising ways. Only a few occupations, such as air traffic control, operate largely around highly regulated communicative procedures and a restricted language repertoire.

Research and Applications

The emphasis on performance competencies has been particularly common in workplace ESP training, English for highly specific situations, and 'shot in the arm' projects of limited duration. The following example illustrates a 'shot in the arm' ESP project in the Middle East based on training target situation performance competencies.

Ball (1994) reports an ESP project developed by the British Council for bank tellers in an Arabic-speaking country. The 3-day ESP course was part of a month-long training program for bank tellers with good knowledge of banking procedures including currency transfers. The ESP course aimed to provide the tellers with English language skills to be able to process currency transfers for non-Arabic-speaking customers. The course targeted two key functions for the bank tellers: to elicit information from the customer in English and to issue a foreign currency draft in English.

Teaching was based around the currency transfer form used in the bank. Instruction involved activities such as eliciting questions used when completing the form (What is the beneficiary's bank? How much do you want to transfer?). It also involved role-plays between bank tellers and customers. The role-plays were videoed and feedback provided by the teachers on aspects of the students' language use, such as grammar, vocabulary, and choice of politeness formula. The trainees were assessed on their ability to perform the two key functions in English and were judged on this by an expatriate employee of the bank. The criterion the expatriate employee used for assessment was: 'If you were doing a currency transaction, would this trainee be able to serve you effectively and efficiently in English?'

TO TEACH UNDERLYING KNOWLEDGE

Concepts

Using a second or foreign language for workplace or study purposes requires not only linguistic proficiency and knowledge but also knowledge and understanding of work-related and disciplinary concepts. According to Douglas (2000), specific-purpose language ability results from interaction between specific-purpose background knowledge and language ability. ESP teaching with preexperienced students (students with limited familiarity with their target workplaces and disciplines) may set out to teach specific purpose background knowledge. The term *underlying competencies* in ESP was used by Hutchinson and Waters (1985) to refer to disciplinary concepts from the students' field of study. They argued that ESP should focus on developing students' knowledge of these disciplinary concepts as well as their language skills. The objective of teaching underlying knowledge can be classified as a cultural knowledge objective, according to Stern's categorization (1992).

Recent proposals have been made for ESP teaching to familiarize students with ways of thinking in their target situations. Hirvela (1997) argues that conventional ESP teaching that has focused on teaching specific-purpose language use and genres has provided information about the surface properties of disciplinary language and rhetoric. However, it has failed to provide necessary information about the 'invisible discourse' (p. 216) of discourse communities—the ways of thinking and frames of reference. These elements are not on the surface of the discourse, but they are essential for producing and understanding it.

The field of professional education recognises the need to introduce learners to ways of thinking. Dinham and Stritter (1986) describe professional education as bringing about a 'change of gestalt that marks the metamorphosis from novice to professional . . . transforming the students' gestalt from confusion to familiarity, so that the student comes to inhabit the professional world' (p. 953).

Research and Applications

Gimenez (2001) reports a cross-cultural study of business negotiation strategies. The study focused on the strategies of negotiators from a range of countries negotiating with an import–export company in the United

Kingdom. The study showed that the negotiations opened with a move termed *establishing the credentials*. In this move, buyers concentrated on their company's current assets and buying power, and sellers concentrated on their company's fixed assets and selling power. However, cross-cultural differences emerged in the strategies buyers and sellers from different cultures used in approaching issues. For example, the Iranian negotiator used the approach of 'extra benefits' as a way of compensating for what the seller did not have, a strategy not used by negotiators from different cultures. The results led Gimenez to make two proposals for teaching negotiations in English for Business Purposes courses. First, teaching should incorporate an exploration of the status-bound behavior of negotiators (whether buyer or sellers). Second, students should be required to role-play negotiations and teachers should use the role-plays as a basis for discussion on cultural differences in strategy choice. These proposals are examples of ESP teaching with a focus on teaching conceptual and cultural knowledge.

Hutchinson and Waters (1985) proposed that the ESP classroom was the appropriate place to introduce students to concepts from their disciplines in addition to the language the students would need to express those concepts. They were led to make this proposal partly by their own teaching situation. They taught ESP courses in the United Kingdom to overseas students. The courses aimed to prepare the students for study in technical colleges in the United Kingdom. Hutchinson and Waters argued that in such cases, ESP teaching needed to play a role in providing the students with background knowledge, termed *underlying competency*. This meant teaching general conceptual subject content alongside language. In Hutchinson and Waters's situation this meant, for example, teaching engineering students about pump systems while teaching language use for describing systems and processes.

TO DEVELOP STRATEGIC COMPETENCE

Concepts

Discussions of strategic competence have appeared in definitions of language ability in the language-testing literature. Douglas (2000) proposes a three-part model of specific-purpose language ability comprising language knowledge (grammatical, textual, functional, and sociolinguistic), background knowledge, and strategic competence (assessment of the external context and engaging a discourse domain). Douglas argues that strategic competence acts as a 'mediator' between the external situational context and the internal language and background knowledge that is needed to respond to the communicative situation (p. 38). Strategic competence is the link between context of situation and language knowledge and can be defined as the means that enables language knowledge and content knowledge to be used in communication.

Teaching oriented toward the development of strategic competence aims to recognise and work from the preexisting knowledge base of the student:

> The ESP teacher, for the most part, does not in any straightforward sense conform to the image of a 'knower.' It is true that he or she possesses specialist knowledge of the target language which the learner is interested in acquiring; he or she may be fortunate enough to possess some familiarity with the subject matter relevant to the learner's area of study or concentration. It is more likely, however . . . that the learner will possess far more knowledge in depth in his or her own specialist field than the teacher. (Early, 1981, p. 85)

Teaching ESP to students who have workplace and professional experience or who have experience in study in their disciplines may aim to develop the students' strategic competence. The intent is to bring to the surface the knowledge of the subject area that the students already have and to create opportunities for the students to actualize this knowledge in the target language (in this case, English).

In the ESP literature, Dudley-Evans and St. John (1998) maintain that ESP learners bring to language learning knowledge of their own specialist field and communication in it. Although this knowledge may be conscious, it is often latent (implicit or tacit knowledge) and thus learners will not be able to control the use of that knowledge. Therefore, 'the ESP teacher's job may be to develop a more conscious awareness so that control is gained' (p. 188). Teaching with this focus can be categorized as having a linguistic knowledge objective, according to Stern's classification (1992).

Research and Applications

In working with postgraduate students from highly specialised fields, the EAP unit at Birmingham University developed a team teaching approach (Dudley-Evans & St. John, 1998). Their aim was to avoid situations in which 'the EAP teacher . . . with a smattering of knowledge in the subject area, and a view of himself as an expert on communication . . . comes to regard himself as an expert—or the expert—on how the subject ought to be taught, and even what the subject ought to be ' (p. 152). The approach involved three parties in teaching: the EAP teacher, the subject specialist, and the students. The role of the teacher was to be a mediator between the language and subject knowledge by providing language needed to express the content.

The following sequence shows an example sequence of instruction.

> Before the team teaching session:
> The subject specialist records a lecture. In this case the subject specialist is a lecturer in highway engineering. The EAP teacher devises a worksheet of questions on the lecture content. The student or students write their responses to the questions.

> The team teaching session:
> A team-taught session is held in which the student(s), the lecturer of highway engineering and the EAP teacher are present. The session focuses on the responses of the student(s) to items on the worksheet items. The subject specialist gives information as needed on points of content and the language teacher helps with any language points arising.

> A number of advantages are given for team teaching:
> • The student(s) have immediate assistance with any difficulties as they arise.
> • Subject specialists find out how effectively they communicate to the students.
> • The EAP teacher gains familiarity with the conceptual matter of the subject and how language is used to represent it.
> • The EAP teacher understands where linguistic difficulties arise in relation to conceptual matter. (Johns & Dudley-Evans, 1985, p. 141).

TO FOSTER CRITICAL AWARENESS

Concepts

Teaching objectives listed in the previous sections are based on a common understanding that the role of ESP is to help students fit into their target academic, professional, or workplace environments. Despite differences among the objectives, all have the overriding goal of enabling students to become accepted members of those target environments, and all have a shared understanding that ESP can best help students attain this end by helping them develop the skills and knowledge they need to produce acceptable language in those environments. Thus conventionally the role of ESP has been construed in terms of helping English language learners meet the demands and expectations of the target environment, to close the gap between the students' present state of skills and knowledge and the level required by members of the target environment. This taken-for-granted understanding has recently come to be challenged and a critical approach proposed in its place. See Hyland and Hamp-Lyons (2002) and Basturkmen and Elder (2004) for overviews of the literature relating to conventional views about the role of EAP and ESP and emerging critical approaches.

A critical approach to ESP questions whether the function of ESP teaching should be exclusively on helping students fit into target situations by teaching them the language, behaviors, or knowledge to act appropriately. Proponents of a critical approach (Benesch, 2001; Pennycook, 1997) challenge the idea that teaching should promote the communicative norms of the target environment and lead students to accept these norms uncritically. Hyland and Hamp-Lyons (2002) report, as a central issue for EAP, the question of whether it is 'the EAP teacher's job to replicate and reproduce existing forms of discourse (and thus power relations) or to develop an understanding of them so that they can be challenged?' (p. 9).

ESP has most often been seen as a pragmatic venture that helps students become familiar with established communicative practices (Allison, 1996, 1998). Benesch (1996) describes critical approaches as a reaction to the pragmatic ESP/EAP perspective that 'changing existing forms is unrealistic whereas promoting them is practical' (p. 736). A critical orientation of ESP has led to the accusation that ESP has been a force for accommodation and conservatism (modifying students to suit established norms in the target environment and maintaining the status quo of those environments). By seeking to prepare non-native speaker students for target discourse communities, ESP may have inadvertently endorsed practices and norms of target environments. Thus, ESP may be in part responsible for the maintenance of norms and practices not all of which are necessarily desirable.

Instruction with the aim of raising students' critical awareness would involve discussing with students how norms and communicative practices in the target environments become established, encouraging students to critique any negative aspects, and making them aware of ways to try to change or modify the situation so as to position themselves better in relation to it. It can be argued that unless teachers raise students' awareness of the negative aspects, they may be choosing compliance for them. This objective can be linked to the cultural knowledge and affective objectives in Stern's (1992) classification. It may be considered an affective objective because teaching seeks to change the way the students feel about themselves and to improve their perceptions of their status in relation to members of target environments and discourse communities.

A potential drawback of leading ESP students to critique the established practices and status quo is that this might result in a situation where doors will be closed to the students. Opponents of critical approaches argue that critical approaches may 'deny students access to the language and discourses they need' (Pennycook, 1997b, p. 265). Pennycook and other proponents of critical approaches argue that this is not the case. Leading students to critique established practices helps them modify the practices to better suit their needs and thus this opens up doors to them, making it easier for them to function in or gain access to their chosen target environments.

Writing on applied linguistics generally, Fairclough (1992) critiques the notion of teaching appropriate language use for two reasons. First, it implies the existence of a culturally homogeneous speech community. In fact, real speech communities, Fairclough argues, demonstrate cultural heterogeneity. Second, it promotes normativity and training. In place of teaching appropriate language use, language education should try to help learners develop critical language awareness. The advantage of such awareness is that learners will be positioned to choose which language practices they wish to engage in and which they wish to modify or reject:

> Critical language awareness . . . should not push learners into oppositional practices which condemn them to disadvantage and marginalisation; it should equip them with the capacities and understanding which are preconditions for meaningful choice and effective citizenship in the domain of language. (Fairclough, 1992, p. 54).

In a discussion of EAP, Coleman (1996) draws attention to the distinction between autonomous and ideological functions of language education. An autonomous view assumes that education has the same function or set of functions in every society, that there is one possible set of behaviors appropriate for all systems of higher educations that can be used to evaluate the adequacy of any educational enterprise. An ideological view assumes that the functions are culturally embedded. Each society or culture creates its own function and there are no 'universally relevant roles' (p. 2). The function or set of functions differs according to societies. Coleman critiques EAP for conventionally adhering to an autonomous view in which teaching has tended to assume the ubiquity of patterns, skills, and procedures. When EAP course participants (students and academics from other parts of the world) are found not to share these, EAP has tended to fault the participants for thinking in 'illogical,' 'vague,' and 'unclear ways' and failing to give regards to diverse ways of thinking (p. 8).

The emergence of critical perspectives has led to discussion in the world of ESP. This is illustrated in the debate about EAP between Allison and Pennycook that appeared in *English for Specific Purposes Journal* (Allison, 1996, 1998; Pennycook, 1997b). Allison (1996) argued that the role of EAP had always been and should continue to be essentially pragmatic. Pennycook (1997b) challenged the conventional role of EAP and accused EAP of 'vulgar' pragmaticism in that it had focused almost exclusively on the everyday concerns of developing courses and materials and needs analysis.

EAP, argued Pennycook, had failed to make ethical or aesthetic choices and distinguish between good and bad communicative practices in target environments. It had uncritically accepted the communicative practices as the objective facts of the situation. Pennycook accused EAP of being conformist and assuming a conservative attitude toward the dominant academic system. In effect, it had played a role in upholding the status of dominant academic in-groups. EAP needed to look beyond the everyday concerns of course preparation and needs analysis (*how* questions) and ask broader political and cultural questions, such as what should be done and why (*what* and *why* questions). It needed to consider social and political issues and no longer uncritically accept the existing states of affairs, implicit or explicit standards, conventions, norms, rules, and communicative practices of academia. EAP needed to reexamine its view of science and technology as a neutral supracultural entity transcending local contexts and consider whose version of science and technology was being offered to students. It needed to reexamine the role of EAP teaching and move away from seeing English classes as mere adjuncts to disciplinary subjects and toward making English classes sites for change and resistance.

Research and Applications

EAP studies have set out to investigate diverse ways of thinking in the attempt to move away from 'autonomous' views of academic values. Jin and Cortezzi (1996) investigated the understandings of Chinese postgraduate students in the United Kingdom of academic work. Bloor and Bloor (1991) investigated the writing problems of non-native speaker students in an academic writing program in a U.K. university in relation to norms in the students' home cultures. Cadman (1997) explored the difficulties faced by a small group of international students writing humanities and arts theses in an Australian university. Cadman traced the way the students positioned themselves in relation to the claims they made. She found links between the positioning the students took and the identity of 'the student' in their home cultures.

Benesch (1996) reports on her implementation of critical needs analysis and rights analysis in a paired ESL writing/psychology class in the United States. Benesch argues the need for EAP to have a dual focus—the conventional focus of helping students develop linguistic skills for academic work and a new focus on helping students develop linguistic, social, and cultural critical awareness. Benesch critiques conventional needs analysis in ESP for having been concerned only to identify the elements in the target situation as the basis of curriculum development and for being biased toward institutional, in-group wishes. Needs analysis, she argues, has falsely purported to be neutral and to be simply providing objective taxonomies of necessary skills. In fact, these taxonomies of needs have a hidden ideological basis (the representation of institutional wants). Benesch's needs analysis differed from conventional analyses. It focused on the students' perspectives of needs and was used to explore options for transforming the target situation: 'Critical needs analysis assumes that institutions are hierarchial and that those at the bottom are often entitled to more power than they have. It seeks areas where greater equality might be achieved' (Benesch, 1996, p. 736).

Benesch's study revealed that the students found the amount of reading required in one of their psychology papers unmanageable. This led Benesch to provide conventional EAP support in the form of classroom reading skills activities and to try to improve the situation by arranging for the psychology professor to visit the EAP class for a discussion on one of the topics covered in the psychology curriculum. In addition, Benesch attempted to raise the students' social awareness and transform their perceptions of themselves. At the time, elections for governor of New York were being held. Benesch used this opportunity to have the students in her EAP class to write letters to the candidates. In the letters, the students questioned proposals for cutting educational funding, proposals that would directly affect them. In these ways, the EAP course was used to involve the students in political and social processes.

A second study by Benesch (1999) aimed to identify how the students in the paired ESL writing/psychology class asserted their rights in relation to the requirements of a psychology course. Benesch observed the interaction in the psychology lectures. She noted the ways the students resisted the unilateral power of the psychology professor with questions and complaints (such as the speed of the psychology lectures and the lack of reading assignments), and with silence. With the aim of getting the students to act more constructively, Benesch had students in the EAP class write to the professor proposing changes. She thus used EAP teaching to create a means by which the students could modify the situation they faced. Benesch (1999) wrote:

> I believe EAP can help students fulfil certain academic expectations while challenging others. . . . Needs analysis reveals institutional requirements and expectations; rights analysis reveals possibilities for change. The starting point for EAP can be the institutional requirements but a vision of student engagement can provide the momentum for change. This dual focus of compliance and resistance allows students to choose which aspects they want to accept and which they might challenge. (p. 326)

SUMMARY

This chapter examined a range of objectives in ESP teaching. ESP courses are often based on different combinations of objectives, with some courses giving more emphasis to some objectives than others. This may reflect the outlook of the teachers, course designers, and institutions involved.

Examination of objectives for teaching ESP led to discussion of what is the legitimate business of ESP. Until very recently, it was taken for granted that ESP was an essentially pragmatic endeavor focused on helping students enter their chosen target workplace, professional, or academic environments. The task of ESP was construed as investigating these environments and analyzing students' needs in relation to them. It was assumed that the demands of the target environment were fixed, and these were represented as the facts of the matter. The role of ESP was to help students meet these demands. However, this conventional outlook on ESP has been challenged. Those advocating a critical role for ESP teaching wish to offer a different type of help. They argue that the demands of the target environment can and sometimes should be adapted to better meet the needs of nonnative speaker would-be members. ESP teaching should work to encourage these would-be members to change the target situation to better suit their needs. Thus ESP teaching should help students realise that target demands may be up for negotiation and that they have a role to play in taking action to help this come about.

QUESTIONS FOR DISCUSSION AND PROJECTS

1. Examine the statement of aims and objectives for two ESP or EAP courses targeting similar students. How comparable are the courses in their teaching objectives?
2. What role do the teaching objectives described in this chapter play in your own teaching? Are some objectives more important than others?
3. Widdowson (1983) critiqued ESP teaching for being a form of training in performance behaviors rather than language education. Widdowson made the following comparisons between general ELT and ESP:

    a. General ELT distinguishes between teaching *aims* (the eventual target behaviors of the students) and *objectives* (the pedagogical means hoped to enable the students to achieve the eventual target behaviors). By contrast, ESP conflates aims and objectives, with the result that courses simply specify where the learner should end up rather than working out the pedagogical means to achieve those ends.

    b. General ELT aims to provide students with a general language capacity. In doing so, it provides the students with the enabling strategies and means to solve independently communication difficulties (often unpredictable in nature) that they will face after completing the language course. By contrast, ESP courses often aim to provide students with a restricted set of language competencies (just enough to function in the target environment). This fails to provide a general language capacity that would allow the students to solve unpredicted communication problems in the future.

Discuss whether you agree with these comparisons and the notion that ESP can be a form of training rather than language education.

4. The English for Bank Tellers course described earlier was an example of a course oriented to developing performance competencies. It involved students with existing background knowledge and operational skills of bank telling. Do you agree that attempts by ESP to teach language for performance competencies may be fruitless if the background knowledge is missing?

5. The objective of teaching underlying competencies implies that the ESP teacher has some knowledge of concepts or culture in the target workplace, professional, or academic environments. It also implies that the ESP teacher is able to teach this kind of knowledge and can do so alongside language teaching. In which circumstances might this be true? In which areas of ESP or EAP would you feel competent to teach disciplinary concepts or cultural content as well as language?

6. To what extent have critical approaches influenced your own teaching situation? Do you consider critical approaches to ESP to be desirable?

FURTHER READING

- Waters and Waters (2001) argue that EAP can usefully teach 'study competence' (cognitive and affective capacity for study) as well as study skills.
- Dudley-Evans (2001) discusses the role of the EAP teacher in team teaching with subject specialists.
- Ferguson (1997) explores the role of subject-specialist knowledge in ESP teaching and ESP teacher education.
- Douglas (2000) provides an in-depth discussion of the role of background knowledge and strategic competence in assessment of specific-purposes language ability.
- Pennycook (2003) provides an overview of critical approaches in Applied Linguistics.
- Benesch (1996, 1999) argues for a critical approach to EAP and describes how she implemented this approach in her own teaching situation.
- Harwood and Hadley (2004) compare the objectives of critical and pragmatic approaches to the teaching of academic writing.

III

GENERAL

This page intentionally left blank

Synthesis

The previous chapters of this book focused on different aspects of the framework for analysis of ESP introduced in chapter 2. This chapter brings together these aspects and presents the complete framework. A further aim is to demonstrate an analysis of two ESP teaching projects (an on-site English for workplace needs course in the Middle East and a university-based EAP course in United Kingdom) using the framework.

REINTRODUCING THE FRAMEWORK

The opening chapters of this book argued the need for a framework for analysis of ESP. The argument was based on the observation that much of the literature in ESP has described language use in specific disciplines or work areas, or reported particular teaching projects. It was argued that a framework for analysis of the various ideas and options in ESP was needed. It would allow various ESP teaching and research projects to be compared. In the chapters of the book, various components of the framework have been described and illustrated. Figure 11.1 shows these components, complete with the options and ideas described in the book.

The framework can be used to analyze and compare ESP projects. When using it in this way, certain caveats should be borne in mind:

• ESP teachers and course developers do not necessarily set out to design lessons and courses according to a predetermined view of language, learning, or teaching. Courses may develop over time and be contributed to by different course developers and teachers. In such cases, the rationale for the course emerges and may change over time.

• Not all ESP projects involve statements of the ideas on which they are based. The ideas may need to be inferred from the approaches used in them.

149

		Sentence grammar
	systems	Text patterns
Language		
		Speech acts
	uses	Genres
		Social interaction
		Lexico-semantic mappings

	conditions	Acculturation
		Input & interaction
Learning		
		Intramental
	processes	Social

		Input
	methodologies	Input-output
		Output
		Output-input
Teaching		
		To reveal subject specific language use
		To train performance behaviours
	objectives	To develop underlying competencies
		To foster strategic competence
		To develop critical awareness

FIG. 11.1.   Reintroducing the framework.

• Although some ESP projects are espoused to specific ideas about the nature of language, learning, and teaching (for example, some research projects investigate discipline- or workplace-specific language use in line with one particular language theory), other projects may involve a mix of ideas.

• The components of the framework are not necessarily equally important in individual cases. Some ESP courses involve definite ideas about the type of language content that should be provided but not about the types of learning activities that should be used. Some reports of research into discipline- or workplace-specific language use include discussion of how the findings can be used for teaching and learning, but not all do.

USING THE FRAMEWORK

This section of the chapter demonstrates how the framework was used to analyse and compare two different ESP teaching projects. Case One is an on-site ESP project for a finance center developed by the British Council in Kuwait. The 'data' for the analysis included the course description and outline, sample teaching materials, tests, postcourse evaluations, and reports prepared by the British Council in Kuwait. The second case is an EAP course developed at Birmingham University, UK. The 'data' for the second case included a face-to-face interview with the course convenor, the course outline, and a selection of instructional materials from the course that were discussed in this interview.

Case One

The first case is an on-site ESP teaching project run in 1999 by the British Council in Kuwait for five members of the Kuwait Finance Centre (KFC). The students had a range of English language proficiency levels. The class met at KFC three times a week for 2 hours each day. Two teachers taught the course.

The course objectives were stated as: To enable trainees to develop their speaking, listening, reading and writing skills, and to extend their range of language structures and vocabulary in the field of finance and investment so that they can:

• Participate in meetings, discussions, question and answer sessions.
• Understand financial and investment terminology and explain the market situation in Kuwait and globally.
• Make presentations on aspects of finance and investment.

- Listen to radio and television programs, and take part in international seminars and conferences on finance and investment.

- Write financial and investment reports.

- Constantly update their knowledge and read extensively, assimilating information from a wide range of published materials on finance and investment so that they can apply this in their work and be more effective when discussing their work and related issues with colleagues.

- Communicate both face to face and on the telephone, by fax, and e-mail.

- Socialize with colleagues.

The course description includes statements about the ideas of learning on which the course was based:

> The basic principle of our teaching and training is that the most effective learning takes place when language is introduced and practised in realistic contexts. Genuine team communication between participants through group work, role-play and simulation assists in language acquisition and helps develop confidence in the learner. This encourages the participants to be motivated and succeed in their learning.

The instruction was organized into three stages of approximately 50 hours each. Stage Three focused on two main areas: financial vocabulary on topics such as company finance, bankruptcy, shares and investment, and the development of spoken fluency in business contexts such as participating in discussions and meetings, giving presentations, and receiving visitors at work. Example teaching activities from this stage are:

- Students read or listen to authentic texts, such as official annual financial reports, newspaper articles about finance, and televised business news reports. Comprehension tasks such as deciding whether statements about the text are true or false are provided. Following the comprehension tasks, the teacher uses the text to focus on vocabulary used in financial reporting.

- The teacher leads the class in brainstorming language used in meetings. The various speech acts or functions used in meetings (such as agreeing and interrupting) are discussed and possible linguistic realisations presented. (See Fig. 11.2).

The students were assessed on their knowledge of financial reporting vocabulary. One assessment task required students to match words and definitions (such as, antitrust = laws making monopolies illegal).

Analysis. A good deal of attention in this course was given to descriptions of language use. Two types of description were given: description of speech acts and vocabulary items used in financial reporting, and the concepts they carried. The course description contained an explicit statement concerning ideas of learning. It was stated that learning was believed to be most effective when it occurred in groups or teams. This indicated a leaning toward social interaction views of learning. The course objectives were stated in terms of language skills and helping students develop specific work-related competencies, such as writing financial reports. This indicated that the teacher-course developers saw the function of the course in terms of training target performance behaviors. This was not surprising given the fact that the course was a short-term, shot-in-the-arm project that was taught on-site and had been convened at the behest of the employers. As only a limited amount of teaching material was available for analysis, I am hesitant to identify a teaching methodology for this course. The materials I was able to examine were input-based (input alone or input–output). It is possible that other methodological options were used on the course. No particular ideas about the conditions needed for learning were evident. The analysis is shown in Fig. 11.3.

Case Two

The second case is an academic writing course for scientists and engineers provided by the English for International Students Unit at Birmingham University, UK. The Unit offers a number of courses to international students. The courses include academic writing for arts, social science, education and law, exam skills, and thesis writing. The Unit also offers other types of support, such as consultations with individual students to discuss the particular pieces of writing they are preparing for their content classes and computer self-access learning facilities. The analysis of this course is made on the basis of an interview held in 2001 with the convenor of the course, Tony Dudley-Evans (former editor of the *English for Specific Purposes Journal*) and the samples of instructional materials that he brought with him to the interview.

The academic writing course for scientists and engineers was (at the time of the interview) a noncredit-bearing, one-semester course that met once a week. Most of the students were postgraduates. The course description specified its aims as to help students with report writing (how to write abstracts, introductions, discussions of results, and conclusions) and common problems of writing essays (how to organize ideas and arguments). The course was held in a large lecture theatre, and the instruction (according to the convenor) was in the form of a 'lecture about academic writing with interludes for practice activities.'

MEETINGS IN ENGLISH

(starting)
Right I think we should begin
Ok let's start

(assigning roles)
~ is going to
~ I'd like you to...
Could you ~ tell us about?

(setting objectives)
Our aim today is..
What we've got to do today is...

(requesting opinions)
What's your opinion/view?
What do you think?

(giving opinions)
As far as I can see...
It seems to me that...

(agreeing)
Yes I agree with you
Absolutely
I couldn't agree more

(disagreeing)
Well up to a point but ...
I'm sorry but I really can't agree....

(moving forward)
Let's move on..
Can we now go on to..?

(finishing)
We're running out of time
OK let's finish

(final points)
Does anyone have anything else to say?
Is there any other business?

(summing up)
Let me sum up
Let's recap what we've....

(making recommendations)
I (recommend/suggest/propose) we..

(returning to the main point)
Anyway as I was saying..
Well let's get back to ...

(asking a question)
What I'd like to know is..
About your 2nd point ...

(accepting an interruption)
Yes of course go ahead
Yes, please do

(interrupting)
Sorry to interrupt but
Can I just ask as question/
Say something?

(refusing an interruption)
Actually can I come back to that?
Sorry but can I just finish?

FIG. 11.2.   Notes for the lesson Meetings in English. Reprinted with permission from the British Council, Kuwait.

FIG. 11.2 (continued)

155

Language	systems	Sentence grammar
		Text patterns
	uses	Speech acts +
		Genres
		Social interaction
		Lexico-semantic mappings +
Learning	conditions	Acculturation
		Input & interaction
	processes	Intramental
		Social +
Teaching	methodologies	Input
		Input-output
		Output
		Output-input
	Objectives	Reveal the truth about subject specific language
		Train performance behaviours +
		Develop underlying competencies
		Foster strategic competence
		Develop critical awareness

FIG. 11.3.   Analysis of Case One.

The convenor described the main focus of instruction as informing students about what types of information should be included in their writing and how they should be organised. The focus was also on 'social or cultural positioning' (highlighting the kind of information that is appropriate in scientific or engineering writing and what stance student researchers should take in presenting it). The course was organized around particular genres and various elements in them (research reports, presentation of results, and discussion of results).

The course outline did not include an explicit statement about ideas of learning or methodology. The convenor commented that there had been little conscious consideration of these questions in developing and running the course over the years. However, it was possible to make some inferences about these on the basis of the instructional materials provided (see examples of this material shown in Fig. 11.4 and Fig. 11.5). In Case Two a good deal of instructional material was provided, and the materials in Fig. 11.4 and Fig. 11.5 are fairly representative of the type of instruction in general. The materials focus on presenting results in research reports. The teacher leads the class in analysis of the sequential organization of information in terms of moves (the comment on the results and counterarguments) and on linguistic realisations of the moves (drawing attention to results through 'as' clauses). The activities provided indicate a view of learning that is intramental and conscious. Instruction aims to draw the students' conscious attention to features in the language input. They also indicate an incremental view of learning—the students' attention is drawn to discrete items of language with the idea that the students will eventually use the parts together. A view of learning as an individual activity is indicated. Students are not required to interact with each other in the activities. The methodology appears to be based on an input–output teaching strategy. There is a great deal of attention given to analysis and explication of language features in the input, and this is followed by practice activities in which students are to use the information about moves and language realisations in production work.

Analysis. This course targeted the development of genre knowledge. It aimed to help students become more explicitly aware of genre conventions in academic scientific and engineering writing. Thus its role was to reveal academic language use. It appeared to function to an extent in developing strategic competence. The course drew on the students' tacit knowledge of writing in science and engineering. The convenor described the use of techniques in instruction to elicit the students' implicit genre knowledge. Recall that it was at Birmingham University that the team-teaching approach for highway engineers reported in Dudley-Evans and St. John (1998) was developed. Figure 11.6 (p. 163) shows an analysis of Case Two based on the framework.

SUMMARY

This chapter brought together the various ideas about language, learning and teaching ESP discussed in earlier chapters and presented a 'complete picture' of the Framework for Analysis of ESP. The framework was then used as a point of reference for the analysis and description of two ESP teaching projects. This enabled some key ideas underpinning the two projects to be identified. It is arguably the ideas basis of ESP programs, as well as situational and contextual factors (such as the type of learner and subject area), that make them distinctive.

The case analyses revealed two distinctive versions of ESP. The first case was a shot-in-the-arm, on-site ESP project. It involved a well-articulated notion of learning through interaction. The language content was speech-act-based, with attention given also to key lexical items in financial reporting and the concepts the items carry in that field. The course functioned to train specific target situation performance competences. The second project was based on a clearly articulated alignment to genre-based descriptions of language use. A view of learning was not articulated, but a fairly conventional view of learning as an individual activity involving an emphasis

PRESENTING AND DISCUSSING YOUR RESULTS

Handling numerical data is an integral part of scientists and engineers work. Results are presented as graphs diagrams and charts, and are always accompanied by written information. We are going to look at the kind of information you provide as a writer and the language you use.

---

1. DRAWING THE READER'S ATTENTION TO YOUR RESULTS

The graph and text below are part of a report on world fish consumption.

a) <u>What information does the writer provide in the text?</u>

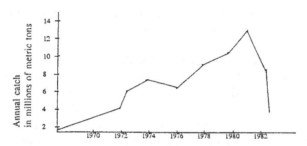

Fig. 1   The Worldwide Anchovy Catch 1970-1982.

As shown in Figure 1, the anchovy catch grew steadily in the seventies, and reached a maximum of thirteen million metric tons in 1980. However, in 1982 there was a dramatic fall off in the catch and only 4,000,000 tons were harvested. There are two likely reasons for this sudden change. Coastal waters had warmed up, and this probably adversely affected the anchovies survival and reproduction. Secondly biologists had warned that the catch should not be more than 10 million tons per annum. This limit was exceeded in the two years before the 1982 disaster.

> Pattern of information to accompany a graph:
>
> *
>
> *
>
> *
>
> *

FIG. 11.4. Drawing the reader's attention to your results. Prepared by T. Dudley-Evans and M. St. John (2001). Reprinted by permission.

The writer draws the reader's attention to the graph with the expression "As shown in Figure 1..."

i)   This type of AS clause functions as a linking device and therefore is usually placed at the beginning
        of the sentence. It connects the main part or idea of the sentence to the following:

eg.   In this experiment, ... , the effects of conditioning seem largely confined to the context where it was
        established. The results of the 2nd experiment help to explain why. <u>As can be seen in the table</u>,
        there is only one change in the design...

ii)   You should also note that an "as" clause is followed by a comma and <u>not</u> by 'that'. We say:

                As shown in the diagram, production has risen ...
                The diagram shows that production has risen...

Other linking "as" clauses can refer to what has been written (or spoken) earlier:

                As stated ...,   As demonstrated ...,   As mentioned ...

iii)   You may have noticed that the structure of these linking "as" clauses is unusual in that they have no
        subjects. Compare:

        a)   When it has been proved, the theory will be of practical importance.
        b)   As [has been] proved, the theory will be of practical importance.

Why is the structure of b different to that of a?

What "As" expressions can you form from the information below?

verb	preposition	noun phrase
show		the beginning
see	in	the following formula
state	by	my last lecture
mention	at	the footnote
demonstrate	from	a comparison
explain		the previous chapter

FIG. 11.4 *(continued)*

on the role of explicit knowledge and language analysis was inferred on the
basis of the instructional materials provided.

QUESTIONS FOR DISCUSSION AND PROJECTS

1. Investigate and write a report on an on-going ESP teaching project.
   Describe the context and the ideas on which the program is based.
   To describe the context provide information about the participants

8.   ESTABLISHING THE VALIDITY OF RESULTS

Your results have no validity of themselves; you have to establish their validity and persuade the readers of that validity. Only then can you go on to make claims for any interpretation of them.

There are several ways in which you can establish the validity of your results, and we have looked at the language of some of them (*).

i)   by commenting on and justifying your procedure
ii)   by citing others (i.e. comparison with previous research)*
iii)   by evaluating the quality of data (accuracy)*
iv)   by guarded/hedged interpretation/hypotheses*
v)   by commenting on difficulties, discrepancies, baffling results*

So a discussion of results section will contain a series of results and comment moves. With additional moves a pattern similar to that may be found:

DISCUSSION OF RESULTS

```
                        Background information

                   ┌─  Reference to a set of results

Cyclical            │   Factual statements re those results
pattern             │
which               │                      ┌ justification of procedure
may                 │                      │ comparison with others
occur               │   Comment on the results  accuracy/quality
several             │                      │ discrepancies + explanation
times              └─                      └ Hypothesis/hedged specific interpretation

                        Counter arguments

                        Recommendations/suggestions

                        Suggestions for future research

                        Conclusion (possibly a separate section)
```

Exercise

a)   Look at the extracts which give comments on results. Identify which category each comment falls into.

1.   In agreement with Handler and Klei (6) we have found splitting of DPN by brain more rapid than by kidney.

2.   Emphasis has been given to the DPN values, since these are considered most precise.

FIG. 11.5.   Establishing the validity of results. Prepared by T. Dudley-Evans
and M. St. John (2001). Reprinted by permission.

3. The foregoing data indicate that the predominant mechanism of DNP splitting in rabbit kidney is by pyrophosphate action.

4. We may infer that conformational changes ... expose the ... to tryptic cleavage.

5. In view of this trend toward more efficient use of ATP at levels nearer the physiological range of ..., measurements were made at ...

6. It is not clear that these variations among the supercoiled molecules can be explained by differences in their content of SS regions or their contamination with SSDNA.

7. Values obtained both by enzymatic and ion exchange chromatographic analyses were in good agreement.

8. The enzymatic properties of the nearly homogeneous dUPTase are ... similar to those reported for the partially purified preparations.

9. This prolonged and extensive autolysis increased the specific activity of the enzyme preparation approximately 10-fold with little loss in yield.

10. ... this suggests a participation of metal ions in the structure or function of the enzyme.

b) Underline all the expressions which the writers have hedged. Could you make any of the claims stronger? How would you make the claims more tentative?

Current claim	Strengthened	More tentative

Exercise

Now look at these longer extracts and identify the moves the writer is making.

Extract A

1. In our study, ... , pH was rarely high during cimetidine treatment. The 52% reduction in hydrogen-
2. ion concentration with full-dose cimetidine, though less than the reductions reported on some studies
3. (eg that of Pounter et al 23) is similar to that found in other studies (eg that of Burland et al). The
4. response to cimetidine in normal subjects varies considerably between individuals and between sexes

FIG. 11.5 *(continued)*

5. and hence varies from study to study. In our study only 20% and 12% of samples were of pH 4 or
6. greater on full-dose and maintenance treatment, respectively. High bacterial counts consequently were
7. also found rarely, and there were no significant increases in bacterial counts over the 24 hour
8. sampling period during cimetidine treatment; this finding agrees with those of Muscroft et al, who
9. also studied subjects who had fed and fasted.

Move/type of information	Sentence(s)

Extract B

1. There was a very good correlation between testosterone and 5x-DHT in the stroma but not in the
2. epithelium, while, on the other hand, good correlations were observed between androstenedione and
3. 5x-androstenedione in both cell preparations. This result may be a consequence of the fact that 5x-
4. DHT of stromal origin may supplement epithelial concentrations (Cowan et al 1977, 1979). A source
5. of 5x-DHT external to the epithelial cells would tend to disturb any original correlation between
6. testosterone and 5x-DHT in these cells because the metabolism of testosterone to 5x-DHT is
7. irreversible.

Move/type of information	Sentence(s)

FIG. 11.5 *(continued)*

162

Language	systems	Sentence grammar Text
	uses	Speech acts Genres + Social interaction Lexico-semantic mappings
Learning	conditions	Acculturation Input & interaction
	processes	Intramental + Social
Teaching	methodologies	Input Input-output + Output Output-input
	objectives	Reveal the truth about subject specific language + Train performance behaviours Develop underlying competencies Develop strategic competence + Foster critical awareness

FIG. 11.6.   Analysis of Case Two using the framework.

(how many students and teachers are involved, what experience and knowledge they have of the target environments and where the course is held). Also provide information on the course (how long it has been running, why it was set up, who developed the course, course length, the format of instruction and how students are assessed). To describe the ideas on which the course is based, refer to the Framework and the ideas described in preceding chapters. In particular, consider whether there is a language syllabus and if so, what units the syllabus is organized around (patterns of grammar or text, speech acts, genres, lexis), the ideas about learning and teaching methodology that are articulated or can be inferred from the instructional materials, and the functions of ESP teaching toward which the program is geared.

This project requires you to collect 'data' for analysis. There are different types of data you can collect including: documents (course outline, statement of aims and objectives, the syllabus, mission statement and statement of teaching philosophy), interviews (with teacher-course developers, the program director and students) and samples of practice (instructional materials, lesson plans and notes, lesson observations and tests or other forms of assessment).

Name of Material	Language focus	Type of language description	Methodology	Ideas about learning	Notes
1 Making claims	Modifying claims	Use – Social Interaction	Input-output	Explicit and intramental	*Examples of modified claims from authentic scientific research article are presented, teacher-led analysis of the language of modification, and why and when scientists need to modify their claims. Students then transform unmodified claims to modified claims in samples of writing.*
2 Ethics in scientific research	N/A	N/A	Input	Implicit, learning through exposure	*A reading passage and students work on comprehension questions about it. Some teacher-led discussion at end.*

FIG. 11.7.   Grid for close analysis of instructional materials.

2. Which has been more important on the ESP courses and programs you have been involved in—specification of what language is to be taught or principles for learning?

3. Prepare a course proposal for a group of ESP students that you might teach in the future. Your proposal needs to include a statement of the situation (hypothetical), the ideas on which you would base the course, and a sample lesson plan or piece of instructional material:

   • Statement of situation—How long would the course be? Who would teach the course? Who are the students and what kind of ESP course do they require (pre-experience, during experience or post-experience). What is their level of proficiency in English? What needs analysis procedures would you conduct?

   • Ideas—What is your view of language learning in ESP? Decide which ideas to base your course on. Refer to the Framework as a guide.

   • Sample Lesson Plan or Instructional Material—Design either a lesson or a piece of material to demonstrate how you would put your ideas into practice.

4. Make a close analysis of the instructional materials used in one unit of an ESP or EAP course. Use the grid shown in Fig. 11.7 as a guide.

   What is the main focus of the unit? What types of language description, ideas about learning or methodology are incorporated?

5. Is it important for a group of learners to be aware of the ideas on which their course of study is based? If you think it is important, describe activities you could devise to familiarise a new ESP class with the ideas about language, learning or teaching behind the course they are about to study.

FURTHER READING

- Smoak (2003) provides a personal account of her experiences teaching ESP in which she discusses the various ideas that have influenced her.
- Opting for new ideas in language teaching is one thing but implementing them is another. Markee's book (1997) about curricular innovation examines theory and practice in the implementation of change in language education programs. Lamie (2004) proposes a model of curriculum innovation and describes attempts made by EFL teachers in Japan to introduce changes in methods of teaching.
- Littlejohn (1998) discusses the topic of materials evaluation and proposes a set of objective, analytical procedures that can be followed. Ellis (1998) argues the need to evaluate materials before, during, and after use.
- Murray (2002) discusses problems related to the definition of ideas in language teaching.

This page intentionally left blank

References

Adam, C., & Artemeva, N. (2002). Writing instruction in English for academic purposes (EAP) classes: Introducing second language learners to the academic community. In A. M. Johns (Ed.), *Genre in the classroom* (pp. 179–196). Mahwah, NJ: Lawrence Erlbaum Associates.

Allison, D. (1996). Pragmatist discourse and English for academic purposes. *English for Specific Purposes Journal, 16*(4), 85–103.

Allison, D. (1998). Response to Pennycook: Whether, why and how? *English for Specific Purposes Journal, 17*(3), 313–316.

Allison, D. (1999). Key concepts in ELT: Genre. *English Language Teaching Journal, 53*(2), 144.

Anderson, J. (1980). *Cognitive psychology and its implications.* New York: Freeman.

Anderson, J. (1983). *The architecture of cognition.* Cambridge, MA: Harvard University Press.

Auerbach, E. R. (1995). The politics of the ESL classroom: Issues of power in pedagogical choices. In R. Tollefson (Ed.), *Power and inequality in language education* (pp. 9–33). Cambridge: Cambridge University Press.

Austin, J. L. (1962). *How to do things with words.* Cambridge, MA: Harvard University Press.

Badger, R., & White, G. (2000). A process genre approach to teaching writing. *English Language Teaching Journal, 54*(2), 153–160.

Ball, D. (1994). *Language engineering: With special reference to the banking sector.* Unpublished masters dissertation, Aston University, Birmingham.

Barber, C. L. (1985). Some measurable characteristics of modern scientific prose. In J. Swales (Ed.), *Episodes in ESP* (pp. 1–16) Hemel Hempstead: Prentice Hall. (original work published in 1962)

Bardovi-Harlig, K. H. (1990). Do language learners recognize pragmatic violations? Pragmatic versus grammatical awareness in instructed L2 learning. *Teaching English to Speakers of Other Languages Quarterly, 32*(2), 233–259.

Bardovi-Harlig, K. H. (2001). Evaluating the empirical evidence: Grounds for instruction in pragmatics? In K. R. Rose & G. Kasper (Eds.), *Pragmatics in language teaching* (pp. 13–32). Cambridge: Cambridge University Press.

Basturkmen, H. (1998a). Refining procedures: A needs analysis project at Kuwait University. *English Teaching Forum, 36*(4), 2–9.

Basturkmen, H. (1998b). Showing attitude: Uses of hedging in academic speaking. *New Zealand Studies in Applied Linguistics, 4,* 49–67.

Basturkmen, H. (1999). Discourse in MBA Seminars. *English for Specific Purposes Journal, 18*(1), 63–80.

Basturkmen, H. (2003). Specificity and ESP course design. *Regional English Language Council Journal, 34*(1), 48–63.

Basturkmen, H., & Elder, C. (2004). The practice of LSP. In A. Davies & C. Elder (Eds.), *The handbook of applied linguistics* (pp. 672–694). Oxford: Blackwell.

Basturkmen, H., & Lewis, M. (2002). Learner perspectives of success in an EAP writing course. *Assessment in Second Language Writing, 8,* 31–46.

Bazerman, C. (1988). *Shaping written knowledge: The genre and activity of the experimental article in science.* Madison: University of Wisconsin Press.

Beaugrande, R. (1997). Theory and practice in Applied Linguistics: Disconnection, conflict, or dialectic? *Applied Linguistics, 18,* 279–313.

Benesch, S. (1996). Needs analysis and curriculum development in EAP: An example of a critical approach. *Teaching English to Speakers of Other Languages Quarterly, 30*(4), 723–738.

Benesch, S. (1999). Rights analysis: Studying power relations in an academic setting. *English for Specific Purposes Journal, 18*(4), 313–327.

Benesch, S. (2001). *Critical English for Academic Purposes: Theory, politics and practice.* Mahwah, NJ: Lawrence Erlbaum Associates.

Benson, M. (1994). Lecture comprehension in an ethnographic perspective. In J. Flowerdew (Ed.), *Academic listening: Research perspectives* (pp. 181–198). Cambridge: Cambridge University Press.

Berkenkotter, C., & Huckin, T. N. (1993). Re-thinking genre from a socio-cognitive perspective. *Written Communication, 4,* 475–509.

Bhatia, V. J. (1982). *An investigation into formal and functional characteristics of qualifications in legislative writing and its application to English for academic legal purposes.* Unpublished doctoral dissertation, Aston University, Birmingham, England.

Bhatia, V. J. (1993). *Analysing genre: Language use in professional settings.* London: Longman.

Bishop-Petty, A., & Engel, R. (2001). *Teaching ESP through user-friendly study guides.* Paper presented at TESOL Convention, St. Louis, MO.

Blaikie, N. (1995). *Approaches to scientific enquiry.* Oxford: Polity Press.

Bloor, M. (1998). English for Specific Purposes: The preservation of the species. *English for Specific Purposes Journal, 17*(1), 47–66.

Bloor, M., & Bloor, T. (1986). *Languages for specific purposes: Practice and theory* (occasional paper no. 19). Dublin: Trinity College.

Bloor, M., & Bloor, T. (1993). How economists modify propositions. In W. Henderson, T. Dudley-Evans, & R. Backhouse (Eds.), *Economics and language* (pp. 153–169.). London: Routledge.

Bloor, T., & Bloor, M. (1991). Cultural expectations and socio-pragmatic failure in academic writing. In P. Adams, B. Heaton, & P. Howarth (Eds.), *Socio-cultural issues in English for Academic Purposes* (pp. 1–12). London: Macmillan.

Blue, G. M., & Harun, M. (2002). Hospitality language as a professional skill. *English for Specific Purposes, 22*(1), 73–91.

Bosher, S., & Smalkoski, K. (2002). From needs analysis to curriculum development: Designing a course in health-care communication for immigrant students in the USA. *English for Specific Purposes Journal, 21*(1), 59–79.

Boxer, D. P. L. (1995). Problems in the presentation of speech acts in ELT materials: The case of complaints. *English Language Teaching Journal, 49*(1), 44–58.

Brinton, D. M., Snow, M. A., & Wesche, M. B. (1989). *Content-based second language instruction.* New York: Newbury House.

Brown, J. D. (1995). *The elements of language curriculum.* Boston, MA: Heinle & Heinle.

Brown, P., & Levinson, S. L. (1988). *Politeness: Some universals in language usage.* Cambridge: Cambridge University Press.

Cadman, K. (1997). Thesis writing for international students: A question of identity. *English for Specific Purposes Journal, 16*(1), 3–14.

Chambers, F. (1980). A re-evaluation of needs analysis in ESP. *English for Specific Purposes Journal, 1*(1), 25–33.

Chia, H. U., Johnson, R., Chia, H. L., & Olive, F. (1999). English for college students in Taiwan:

A study of the perceptions of English needs in a medical context. *English for Specific Purposes Journal, 18*(2), 107–119.

Clapham, C. (2001). Discipline specificity and EAP. In J. Flowerdew & M. Peacock (Eds.), *Research perspectives in English for Academic Purposes* (pp. 84–100). Cambridge: Cambridge University Press.

Clennell, C. (1999). Promoting pragmatic awareness and spoken discourse skills with EAP classes. *English Language Teaching Journal, 53*(2), 83–91.

Clerehan, R., & Croslin, G. (1998). Minds meeting. In P. Master & D. M. Brinton (Eds.), *New ways in teaching ESP* (pp. 239–241). Alexandria, VA: Teachers of English to Speakers of Other Languages.

Cohen, I. J. (1996). Theories of action and praxis. In B. S. Turner (Ed.), *Social theory* (pp. 111–142). Oxford: Blackwell.

Coleman, H. (1996). *Society and the language classroom.* Cambridge: Cambridge University Press.

Comfort, J. (1995). *Effective presentations.* Oxford: Oxford University Press.

Connor, U. (2002). New directions in contrastive rhetoric. *Teaching English to Speakers of Other Languages Quarterly, 36*(4), 493–510.

Cook, G. (1989). *Discourse.* Oxford: Oxford University Press.

Cook, V. (1997). Second language learning and language teaching. London: Arnold.

Corder, S. Pit (1993). *Introducing applied linguistics.* London: Penguin. (Original work published 1973)

Coxhead, A. (2000). A new academic wordlist. *Teaching English to Speakers of Other Languages Quarterly, 34*(2), 213–238.

Coxhead, A., & Nation, P. (2001). The specialised vocabulary of English for academic purposes. In J. Flowerdew & M. Peacock (Eds.), *Research perspectives on English for Academic Purposes* (pp. 252–267). Cambridge: Cambridge University Press.

Crandall, E. (1999). *Developing and evaluating pragmatics-focused materials.* Unpublished masters thesis, The University of Auckland.

Crandall, E., & Basturkmen, H. (2004). Evaluating pragmatics-focused materials. *English Language Teaching Journal, 59*(1), 38–49.

Crookes, A. (2001). *An E-commerce web page project.* Paper presented at TESOL Convention, St. Louis.

Devitt, A. J. (1991). Intertextuality in tax accounting: Generic, referential and functional. In C. Bazerman & J. Paradis (Eds.), *Textual dynamics of the professions: Historical and contemporary studies of writing in professional communities* (pp. 336–357). Madison: University of Wisconsin Press.

Dhieb-Henia, N. (2003). Evaluating the effectiveness of metacognitive strategy training for reading research articles in an ESP context. *English for Specific Purposes, 22*(4), 397–417.

Dinham, S., & Stritter, F. (1986). Research on professional education. In M. Wittrock (Ed.), *Handbook of research on teaching* (pp. 952–970). New York: Macmillan.

Donato, R. (2000). Sociocultural contributions to the understanding of foreign and second language classroom learning. In J. Lantolf (Ed.), *Sociocultural theory and second language learning* (pp. 27–50). Oxford: Oxford University Press.

Douglas, D. (2000). *Assessing Language for Specific Purposes.* Cambridge: Cambridge University Press.

Dudley-Evans, T. (1994). Genre analysis: an approach for ESP. In M. Coulthard (Ed.), *Advances in written text analysis* (pp. 219–222). London: Routledge.

Dudley-Evans, T. (2001). Team-teaching in EAP: Changes and adaptations in the Birmingham approach. In J. Flowerdew & M. Peacock (Eds.), *Research perspectives on English for Academic Purposes* (pp. 225–238). Cambridge: Cambridge University Press.

Dudley-Evans, T., & St. John, M. (1998). *Developments in English for Specific Purposes.* Cambridge: Cambridge University Press.

Early, P. (1981). The ESP teacher's role—implications for the 'knower–client' relationship. In *English Language Teaching Document 112 The ESP Teacher: Role, Development and Prospects* (pp. 42–52). London: British Council.

Ellis, R. (1990). *Instructed Second Language Acquisition.* Oxford: Blackwell.

Ellis, R. (1997). *SLA and second language teaching.* Oxford: Oxford University Press.

Ellis, R. (1998). The evaluation of communicative tasks. In B. Tomlinson (Ed.), *Materials development in language teaching* (pp. 217–238). Cambridge: Cambridge University Press.

Ellis, R. (2003). *Task based learning and teaching.* Oxford: Oxford University Press.

Ellis, R., Basturkmen, H., & Loewen, S. (2001) Pre-emptive focus on form in the ESL classroom. *Teaching English to Speakers of Other Languages Quarterly, 35*(3), 407–432.

English Language Centre, Kuwait University. (1997). Materials developed in-house by the English Language Unit Engineering (unpublished resource).

Erlam, R. (2003). Evaluating the relative effectiveness of structured-input and output-based instruction in foreign language learning. *Studies in Second Language Acquisition, 25,* 559–582.

Esteban, A. A., & Canado, M. L. P. (2004). Making the case method work in teaching Business English: A case study. *English for Specific Purposes, 23*(2), 137–161.

Evangelou, E. (1994). *Target needs and learning needs in ESP for nurses.* Unpublished masters thesis, Aston University, Birmingham.

Fairclough, N. (1992). *Critical language awareness.* London: Longman.

Ferguson, G. (1997). Teacher education and LSP: The role of specialized knowledge. In R. Howard & G. Brown (Eds.), *Teacher education for LSP* (pp. 80–89). Clevedon: Multilingual Matters.

Ferguson, G. (2001). If you pop over there: A corpus based study of conditionals in medical discourse. *English for Specific Purposes, 20*(1), 61–82.

Ferris, D. (1998). Students' views of academic aural/oral skills: a comparative needs analysis. *Teaching English to Speakers of Other Languages Quarterly, 32*(2), 289–319.

Ferris, D. (2001). Teaching writing for academic purposes. In J. Flowerdew & M. Peacock (Eds.), *Research perspective on English for Academic Purposes* (pp. 298–314). Cambridge: Cambridge University Press.

Field, J. (1998). Skills and strategies: Towards a new methodology for listening. *English Language Teaching Journal, 52*(2), 110–118.

Flowerdew, J., & Peacock, M. (2001a). The EAP curriculum: Issues, methods and challenges. In J. Flowerdew & M. Peacock (Eds.), *Research perspectives on English for Academic Purposes* (pp. 177–194). Cambridge: Cambridge University Press.

Flowerdew, J., & Peacock, M. (2001b). Issues in EAP: A preliminary perspective. In J. Flowerdew & M. Peacock (Eds.), *Research perspectives on English for Academic Purposes* (pp. 8–24). Cambridge: Cambridge University Press.

Flowerdew, L. (1998). Persuasive proposals. In P. Master & D. M. Brinton (Eds.), *New ways in English for Specific Purposes* (pp. 148–149). Alexandria, VA: Teachers of English to Sepakers of Other Languages.

Flowerdew, L. (2000). Using a genre-based framework to teach organizational structure in academic writing. *English Language Teaching Journal, 54*(4), 369–378.

Flowerdew, L. (2001). *Genre-based materials for engineering students.* Paper presented at TESOL Convention, St. Louis.

Freedman, A. (1999). Beyond the text: Towards understanding the teaching and learning of genres. *Teaching English to Speakers of Other Languages Quarterly, 33*(4), 764–767.

Freeman, Y. S., & Freeman, D. (1989). Whole language approaches to writing with secondary students of English as a second language. In D. Johnson & D. Roen (Eds.), *Richness in writing: Empowering ESL students* (pp. 177–193). New York: Longman.

Funnel, P., & Owen, J. (1992). Delivering and measuring competence. In D. Saunders & P. Race (Eds.), *Aspects of educational training technology: Developing and measuring competence* (pp. 27–32). London: Kogan Page.

Giddens, A. (1979). *Central problems in social theory: Action, structure and contradiction in social analysis.* Berkeley: University of California Press.

Giddens, A. (1984). *The constitution of society.* Cambridge: Polity Press.

Gimenez, J. C. (2001). Ethnographic observations in cross-cultural business negotiations between non-native speakers of English: An exploratory study. *English for Specific Purposes Journal, 20*(2), 169–193.

Graves, K. (1996). *Teachers as course developers.* Cambridge: Cambridge University Press.

Hafner, C. (1999). *Genre, register: A comparative study of writing for academic purposes.* Unpublished masters thesis, University of Auckland.

Halliday, M. A. K. (1973). *Explorations in the functions of language.* London: Edward Arnold.

Harwood, N., & Hadley, G. (2004). Demystifying institutional practices: Critical pragmatism and the teaching of academic writing. *English for Specific Purposes Journal, 23*(4), 355–377.

Hatch, E. (1992). *Discourse and language education.* Cambridge: Cambridge University Press.

Hedge, T. (2000). *Teaching and learning in the language classroom.* Oxford: Oxford University Press.

Henry, A., & Roseberry, R. (1998). An evaluation of a genre-based approach to the teaching of EAP/ESP writing. *Teaching English to Speakers of Other Languages Quarterly, 32*(1), 147–156.

Hirose, K. (2003). Comparing L1 and L2 organizational patterns in argumentative writing of Japanese EFL students. *Journal of Second Language Writing, 12*(2), 181–209.

Hirvela, A. (1997). Disciplinary portfolios and EAP writing Instruction. *English for Specific Purposes Journal, 16*(2), 83–100.

Hoey, M. (1994). Signalling in discourse: a functional analysis of a common discourse patterns in written and spoken English. In M. Coulthard (Ed.), *Advances in written text analysis* (pp. 26–45). London: Routledge.

Hoey, M. (2001). *Textual interaction.* London: Routledge.

Holmes, J. (1983). The structure of teachers' directives. In J. C. Richards & R. W. Schmit (Eds.), *Language and communication* (pp. 89–113). London: Longman.

Holmes, J. (1998). *No joking matter! The function of humour in the workplace.* Australian Linguistics Society, Brisbane University of Queensland.

Holmes, J. (1999). Managing social talk at work: What does the NESB worker need to know? *Teaching English to Speakers of Other Languages Journal 7,* 7–19.

Hopkins, A., & Dudley-Evans, T. (1988). A genre-based investigation of the discussion sections in articles and dissertations. *English for Specific Purposes Journal, 7,* 113–121.

Hopper, P. (1987). Emergent grammar. *Berkeley Linguistics Society, 13,* 139–157.

Huang, J.-Y. (2000). *Description of compliment speech act: A critical analysis of its treatment in ELT materials.* Unpublished masters dissertation, University of Auckland.

Hudson, T. (1991). A content comprehension approach to reading English for science and technology. *Teaching English to Speakers of Other Languages Quarterly, 25*(1), 77–104.

Hutchinson, T., & Waters, A. (1985). ESP at the crossroads. In J. Swales (Ed.), *Episodes in ESP* (p. 177–187) Oxford: Pergamon.

Hutchinson, T., & Waters, A. (1987). *English for Specific Purposes: A learning-centred approach.* Cambridge: Cambridge University Press.

Hyland, K. (1996). Writing without conviction? Hedging in science and research articles. *Applied Linguistics, 17*(4), 433–454.

Hyland, K. (2002a). Specificity revisited: How far should we go? *English for Specific Purposes, 21*(4), 385–395.

Hyland, K. (2002b). *Teaching and researching writing.* Harlow: Longman.

Hyland, K., & Hamp-Lyons, L. (2002). EAP: Isues and directions. *Journal of English for Academic Purposes, 1*(1), 1–12.

Ibrahim, A. (1993). *A case study of the manufacturing industry: The ethnographic way.* Unpublished masters dissertation, Aston University, Birmingham.

Jacoby, S., Leech, D., & Holton, C. (1995). A genre-based developmental investigation writing course for undergraduate ESL science majors. In D. Belcher & G. Braine (Eds.), *Academic writing in a second language* (pp. 351–374). Norwood, NJ: Ablex.

Jasso-Aguilar, R. (1999). Sources, methods and triangulation in needs analysis: A critical perspective in a case study of Waikiki Hotel maids. *English for Specific Purposes Journal, 18*(1), 27–46.

Jin, L., & Cortezzi, M. (1996). This way is very different from Chinese ways: EAP needs and academic culture. *Review of English Language Teaching, 6*(1), 205–216.

Johns, A., & Dudley-Evans, T. (1991). English for specific purposes: International in scope, specific in purpose. *Teaching English to Speakers of Other Languages Quarterly, 25*(2), 297–314.

Johns, A. M. (1997a). English for specific purposes and content based instruction: What is the relationship? In M. A. Snow & D. M. Brinton (Eds.), *The content based classroom* (pp. 363–366). White Plains, NY: Longman.

Johns, A. M. (1997b). *Text, role and context: Developing academic literacies.* Cambridge: Cambridge University Press.

Johns, A. M. (2002). *Genre in the classroom.* Mahwah, NJ: Lawrence Erlbaum Associates.

Johns, T. F., & Dudley-Evans, T. (1985). An experiment in team-teaching of overseas postgraduate students of transportation and plant biology. In J. Swales (Ed.), *Episodes in ESP* (pp. 140–153). Oxford: Pergamon.

Jones-Macziola, S., with White, G. (1998). *Further ahead learner's book.* Cambridge: Cambridge University Press.

Jordan, R. R. (1997). *English for Academic Purposes.* Cambridge: Cambridge University Press.

Kaplan, R. B. (1966). Cultural thought patterns in intercultural education. *Language Learning, 16*, 1–20.

Kasper, G. (2001). Classroom research on interlanguage pragmatics. In R. Rose & G. Kasper (Eds.), *Pragmatics in language teaching* (pp. 33–60). Cambridge: Cambridge University Press.

Kasper, G., & Rose, K. R. (2001). Pragmatics in language teaching. In K. R. Rose, & G. Kasper (Eds.), *Pragmatics in language teaching* (pp. 1–10). Cambridge: Cambridge University Press.

Kasper, L. F. (1997). The impact of content-based instructional programs on the academic progress of ESL students. *English for Specific Purposes, 16*(4), 309–320.

Kirkgoz, Y. (1999). *Knowledge acquisition from L2 specialist texts.* Unpublished doctoral dissertation, Aston University, Birmingham.

Kobayshi, H. (1984). Rhetorical patterns in English and Japanese. *Teaching English to Speakers of Other Languages Quarterly, 18*(4), 737–738.

Krashen, S. D. (1982). *Principles and practice in second language acquisition.* Oxford: Pergamon.

Kurtoglu, N. (1992). *Evidence on the discourse discrepancy between DBE and three discourse communities at METU.* Unpublished masters dissertation, Aston University, Birmingham.

Kusel, P. (1992). Rhetorical approaches to the study and composition of academic essays. *System, 20*(4), 457–460.

Lakoff, G. (1973). Hedges: A study in meaning criteria and the logic of fuzzy concepts. *Journal of Philosophical Logic, 2*, 458–508.

Lamie, J. (2004). Presenting a model of change. *Language Teaching Research, 8*(2), 115–142.

Lantolf, J. (2000). *Sociocultural theory and second language learning.* Oxford: Oxford University Press.

Leech, G. (1983). *Pragmatics.* Cambridge: Cambridge University Press.

Li So-mui, F., & Mead, K. (2000). An analysis of English in the workplace: The communication needs of textile and clothing merchandisers. *English for Specific Purposes Journal, 19*(4), 351–368.

Lightbrown, P. (2000). Classroom SLA research and second language teaching. *Applied Linguistics, 21*(4), 431–462.

Linde, C. (1988). The quantitative study of communicative success: Politeness and accidents in aviation discourse. *Language in Society, 17,* 375–399.

Lindemann, S., & Mauranen, A. (2001). "It's just real messy": The occurrence and function of just in a corpus of academic speech. *English for Specific Purposes, 20,* Supplement 1, 459–475.

Littlejohn, A. (1998). The analysis of language teaching materials: Inside the Trojan horse. In B. Tomlinson (Ed.), *Materials development in language teaching* (pp. 190–216). Cambridge: Cambridge University Press.

Loewen, S., & Basturkmen, H. (2005). Interaction, focus on form and group writing tasks in an EAP classroom. *Journal of Asian Pacific Communication, 15*(1), 171–190.

Long, M. H. (1996). The role of the linguistic environment in second language acquisition. In W. C. Richie & T. K. Bhatia (Eds.), *Handbook of second language acquisition* (pp. 413–468). San Diego: Academic Press.

Long, M. H., & Crookes, G. (1992). Three approaches to task-based syllabus design. *Teaching English to Speakers of Other Languages Quarterly, 26*(1), 27–56.

Lynch, T., & Maclean, J. (2000). Exploring the benefits of task repetition and recycling. *Language Teaching Research, 4*(3), 221–250.

Markee, N. (1997). *Managing curricular innovation.* Cambridge: Cambridge University Press.

Martinez, A. C. L. (2001). Empirical examination of EFL readers' use of rhetorical information. *English for Specific Purposes Journal, 21*(1), 81–98.

Master, P. (1998). Positive and negative aspects of the dominance of English. *Teaching English to Speakers of Other Languages Quarterly, 32*(4), 716–727.

Master, P., & Brinton, D. M. (1998). *New ways in English for Specific Purposes.* Alexandria, VA: TESOL.

McCarthy, M. (1991). *Discourse analysis for language teachers.* Cambridge: Cambridge University Press.

McCarthy, C., & Carter, R. (1994). *Language as discourse.* London: Longman.

McLaughlin, B. (1987). *Theories of second language learning.* London: Arnold.

McLaughlin, B., & Heredia, J. L. C. (1996). Information processing approaches to research on second language acquisition and use. In W. C. Ritchie & T. K. Bhatia (Eds.), *Handbook of second language acquisition* (pp. 213–228). San Diego: Academic Press.

Miller, C. (1984). Genre as social action. In A. Freedman & P. Medway (Eds.), *Genre and the New Rhetoric* (pp. 23–42) London: Taylor & Francis.

Minkoff, P. (1994). *Executive skills.* Hemel Hempstead: Prentice Hall.

Mitchell, R., & Myles, F. (1998). *Second language learning theories.* London: Arnold.

Munby, J. (1978). *Communicative syllabus design.* Cambridge: Cambridge University Press.

Muranoi, H. (2000). Focus on form through interaction enhancement: Integrating formal instruction into a communicative task. *Language Learning, 50*(4), 617–673.

Murray, N. (2002). Ideas, their definition, and their vulnerability. *English Language Teaching Journal, 56*(2), 187–189.

Myers, G. (1989). The pragmatics of politeness in scientific articles. *Applied Linguistics, 10*(1), 1–35.

Nurweni, A., & Read, J. (1998). The English vocabulary knowledge of Indonesian university students. *English for Specific Purposes Journal, 18*(2), 161–175.

Orr, T. (1998). Genre files. In P. Master & D. M. Brinton (Eds.), *New ways in English for Specific Purposes* (pp. 103–105). Alexandria, VA: Teachers of English to Speakers of Other Languages.

Paltridge, B. (2000). *Making sense of discourse.* Gold Coast, Queensland: Antepoedean Educational Enterprises.

Parkinson, J. (2000). Acquiring scientific literacy through content and genre: A theme-based language course for science students. *English for Specific Purposes Journal, 19*(4), 369–387.

Parks, S. (2001). Moving from school to the workplace: Disciplinary innovation, border cross-ings, and the reshaping of a written genre. *Applied Linguistics, 22*(4), 405–438.

Pascal Brown, T. (2001). *Might be worth getting it done then: Directives in a New Zealand factory.* Unpublished masters dissertation, Victoria University of Wellington.

Pascal Brown, T., & Lewis, M. (2002). An ESP project: Analysis of an authentic workplace conversation. *English for Specific Purposes, 22*(1), 93–98.

Pennycook, A. (1997a). Critical applied linguistics and education. In R. Wodak & D. Corson (Eds.), *Encyclopedia of language and education* (Vol. 1, pp. 23–31). Dordrecht: Kluwer.

Pennycook, A. (1997b). Vulgar pragmatism, critical pragmatism, and EAP. *English for Specific Purposes, 16*(4), 253–269.

Pennycook, A. (2003). Critical applied linguistics. In A. Davies & C. Elder (Eds.), *The handbook of applied linguistics* (pp. 784–807). Oxford: Blackwell.

Pica, T. (1988). Interlanguage adjustments as an outcome of NS-NNS negotiated interaction. *Language Learning, 38,* 45–73.

Pica, T., Young, R, & Doughty, C. (1987). The impact of interaction on comprehension. *Teaching English to Speakers of Other Languages Quarterly, 21*(4), 737–758.

Prahbu, N. S. (1987). *Second language pedagogy: A perspective.* Oxford: Oxford University Press.

Quirk, R., Greenbaum, S., Leech, G., & Svartik, J. (1972). *A grammar of contemporary English.* London: Longman.

Richards, J. C. (1990). *The language teaching matrix.* Cambridge: Cambridge University Press.

Richards, J. C., & Rodgers, T. S. (1986). *Approaches and methods in language teaching.* Cambridge: Cambridge University Press.

Riggenbach, H. (1990). Discourse analysis and spoken language instruction. *Annual Review of Applied Linguistics, 11,* 152–163.

Rignall, M., & Furneaux, C. (1997). *Speaking student's book.* Hemel Hempstead: Prentice Hall.

Robinson, P. (1991). *ESP today.* London: Prentice Hall.

Robinson, P., Strong, G., Whittle, J., & Nobe, S. (2001). The development of EAP oral discus-sion ability. In J. Flowerdew & M. Peacock (Eds.), *Research perspectives on English for Academic Purposes* (pp. 347–359). Cambridge: Cambridge University Press.

Roebuck, R. (2000). Subjects speak out: How learners position themselves in a psycholinguis-tic task. In J. Lantolf (Ed.), *Sociocultural theory and second language acquisition* (pp. 79–96). Oxford: Oxford University Press.

Rose, K. R., & Kasper, G. (2001). *Pragmatics in language teaching.* Cambridge: Cambridge Uni-versity Press.

Sager, J., Dungworth, D., & McDonald, P. F. (1980). *English special languages.* Wiesbaden, Ger-many: Brandsetter Verlag.

Sakr, A. (2001). *English for textile and clothing industry.* Paper presented at TESOL Convention, St. Louis.

Samraj, B. (2002). Introductions in research articles: variations across disciplines. *English for Specific Purposes Journal, 21*(1), 1–17.

Santos, V. B. M. (2002). Genre analysis of business letters of negotiation. *English for Specific Purposes Journal, 21*(2), 167–199.

Schmidt, R. (1994). Deconstructing consciousness in search of useful definitions for Applied Linguistics. *AILA (Association Internationale de Linguistique) Review, 11,* 11–26.

Schumann, J. (1978). The acculturation model for second language acquisition. In R. Gingas (Ed.), *Second language acquisition and foreign language learning* (pp. 27–50). Arlington, VA: Centre for Applied Linguistics.

Schumann, J. (1986). Research on the acculturation model for second language acquisition. *Journal of Multilingual and Multicultural Development, 7,* 379–392.

Scollon, R., & Scollon, S. (1995). *Intercultural communication.* Oxford: Blackwell.

Scott, H., & Scott, J. (1984). ESP and Rubik's cube: Three dimensions in course design and materials writing. In J. Swales & H. Mustafa (Eds.), *English for Specific Purposes and the Arab World*. Birmingham: Aston University.

Searle, J. R. (1969). *Speech acts: An essay in the philosophy of language*. Cambridge: Cambridge University Press.

Seedhouse, P. (1999). Task-based interaction. *English Language Teaching Journal, 53*(3), 149–156.

Selinker, L., & Douglas, D. (1985). Wrestling with 'context' in interlanguage theory. *Applied Linguistics, 6*(2), 190–204.

Sengupta, S., Forey, G., & Hamp-Lyons, L. (1999). Supporting effective English communication within the context of teaching and research in a tertiary institute: Developing a genre model for consciousness raising. *English for Specific Purposes Journal, 18*(supplement), S7–22.

Sharwood Smith, M. (1993). Input enhancement in instructed SLA: Theoretical bases. *Studies in Second Language Acquisition, 15*, 165–179.

Silver, M. (2003). The stance of stance: A critical look at ways stance is expressed and modelled in academic discourse. *Journal of English for Academic Purposes, 2*(4), 359–374.

Smoak, R. (2003). What is English for Specific Purposes? *English Teaching Forum, 41*(2), 22–27.

Snow, M. A., & Brinton, D. M. (1997). *The content based classroom*. White Plains, NY: Longman.

Starks-Martin, G. (1998). Listen Up! In P. Master & D. M. Brinton (Eds.), *New ways in English for specific purposes* (pp. 103–105). Alexandria, VA: Teachers of English to Speakers of Other Languages.

Stenstrom, A. (1994). *An introduction to spoken interaction*. London: Longman.

Stern, H. H. (1983). *Fundamental concepts in language teaching*. Oxford: Oxford University Press.

Stern, H. H. (1989). Seeing the wood and the trees. In K. Johnson (Ed.), *The second language curriculum* (pp. 207–221). Cambridge: Cambridge University Press.

Stern, H. H. (1992). *Issues and options in language teaching*. Oxford: Oxford University Press.

Sullivan, P., & Girginer, H. (2002). The use of discourse analysis to enhance ESP teacher knowledge: An example of aviation English. *English for Specific Purposes Journal, 21*(4), 397–404.

Swain, M. (1985). Communicative competence: Some roles of comprehensible output in its development. In S. Gass & C. Maden (Eds.), *Input in Second Language Acquisition* (pp. 235–253). Rowley, MA: Newbury House.

Swain, M. (1998). Focus on form through conscious reflection. In C. Dougherty & J. Williams (Eds.), *Focus on form in classroom Second Language Acquisition* (pp. 64–82). Cambridge: Cambridge University Press.

Swales, J. (1985). *Episodes in ESP*. Oxford: Pergamon.

Swales, J. (1990). *Genre analysis: English in academic and research settings*. Cambridge: Cambridge University Press.

Swales, J. (1998). *Language, science and scholarship*. In the Wei Lun Lecture Series VII, 25–35. Hong Kong: The Chinese University of Hong Kong Press.

Swales, J. (2001). EAP-related research: An intellectual history. In J. Flowerdew & M. Peacock (Eds.), *Research perspectives on English for Academic Purposes* (pp. 42–54). Cambridge: Cambridge University Press.

Swales, J., & Feak, C. B. (1994). *Academic writing for graduate students: Essential tasks and skills*. Ann Arbor: University of Michigan Press.

Tarone, E. S., Dwyer, S., Gillette, S., & Icke, V. (1981). One the use of the passive in two astrophysics articles. *English for Specific Purposes Journal, 1*(2), 123–140.

Tauroza, S. (2001). Second language lecture comprehension research in naturalistic controlled conditions. In J. Flowerdew & M. Peacock (Eds.), *Research perspectives on English for Academic Purposes* (pp. 360–374). Cambridge: Cambridge University Press.

Thomas, J. (1983). Cross-cultural pragmatic failure. *Applied Linguistics, 4*(2), 91–112.

Thomas, J. (1995). *Meaning in interaction.* Harlow, Essex: Longman.

Thursten, J., & Candlin, C. N. (1997). *Exploring Academic English.* Macquarie University: National Centre for Language Teaching and Research.

Thursten, J., & Candlin, C. N. (1998). Concordancing and the teaching of the vocabulary of Academic English. *English for Specific Purposes Journal, 17*(3), 267–280.

Tollefson, J. W. (1991). *Planning language, planning inequality.* New York: Longman.

Tomlinson, B. (1998). *Materials development in language teaching.* Cambridge: Cambridge University Press.

Turner, J. (1996). Cultural values in genre skills: The case of the Fine Arts tutorial. In M. Hewings & T. Dudley-Evans (Eds.), *Evaluation and course design in EAP.* London: Prentice Hall Macmillan in association with the British Council.

Ur, P. (1996). *A course in language teaching.* Cambridge: Cambridge University Press.

van Lier, L. (2000). From input to affordance: Social-interactive learning from an ecological perspective. In J. Lantolf (Ed.), *Sociocultural theory and second language learning* (pp. 245–260). Oxford: Oxford University Press.

van Lier, L. (2002). Ecology, contingency and talk in the postmethod classroom. *New Zealand Studies in Applied Linguistics, 8,* 1–20.

Vassileva, I. (2001). Commitment and detachment in English and Bulgarian academic writing. *English for Specific Purposes Journal, 20*(1), 83–102.

Waters, A., & Waters, M. (2001). Designing tasks for developing study competence and study skills in English. In J. Flowerdew & M. Peacock (Eds.), *Research perspectives on English for Academic Purposes* (pp. 375–389). Cambridge: Cambridge University Press.

Watson Todd, R. (2003). EAP or TEAP? *Journal of English for Academic Purposes, 2*(2), 61–70.

Webber, M. (1983). *Elementary technical English.* Edinburgh: Nelson.

Weber, J. J. (2001). A concordance and genre-informed approach to ESP essay writing. *English Language Teaching Journal, 55*(1), 14–20.

Wesche, M. B. (1993). Discipline-based approaches to language study: Research issues and outcomes. In M. Kruger & F. Ryan (Eds.), *Language and content: Discipline and content-based approaches to language study* (pp. 57–82). Lexington, MA: D. C. Heath.

West, M. (1953). *A general service list of English Words.* London: Longman.

West, R. (1994). Needs analysis in language teaching. *Language Teaching Abstracts,* 1–19.

West, R. (1997). Needs analysis: State of the art. In R. Howard & G. Brown (Eds.), *Teacher education for LSP* (pp. 68–79). Clevedon: Multilingual Matters.

Wharton, S. (1999). *From postgraduate student to published writer: Discourse variation and development in TESOL.* Unpublished doctoral dissertation, Aston University, Birmingham.

White, J. (1998). Getting the learners' attention: A typographical input enhancement study. In C. Doughety & J. Williams (Eds.), *Focus on form in classroom second language acquisition* (pp. 85–113). Cambridge: Cambridge University Press.

White, M. (2003). Metaphor and economics: The case of growth. *English for Specific Purposes, 22*(2), 131–151.

White, R. (1988). *The ELT curriculum.* Oxford: Blackwell.

Widdowson, H. G. (1983). *Learning purpose and language use.* Oxford: Oxford University Press.

Willis, J. (1990). *The lexical syllabus.* London: Collins.

Willis, J. (1998). Concordances in the classroom without a computer: Assembling and exploiting concordances of common words. In B. Tomlinson (Ed.), *Materials development in language teaching* (pp. 44–66). Cambridge: Cambridge University Press.

Winter, E. (1994). Clause relations as information structure: Two basic text structures in English. In M. Coulthard (Ed.), *Advances in written text analysis* (pp. 46–88). London: Routledge.

Xue, G., & Nation, I. S. P. (1984). The university word list. *Language Learning and Communica-tion, 3,* 215–229.

Yates, J., & Orlikowski, W. (1997). Genres of organisational communication: A structurational approach to studying communication and media. In C. G. A. Bryant & D. Jary (Eds.), *Antony Giddens: Critical assessments* (pp. 387–415). London: Routledge.

Zhu, Y. (1997). An analysis of structural moves in Chinese sales letters. *Text, 17*(4), 543–566.

This page intentionally left blank

Author Index

Subject Index

A

Abstracts, 73
Academic writing, 62, 66, 67–68, 107, 153, 156–157
Academic genres, 54, 56–57, 58, 119–121, 143, 153, 156–157
Academic reading skills, 99, 102
Academic speaking, 50, 62, 78–80, 92, 93–95, 100–101, 117–118, 128, 130–131
Acculturation, 85–90, 96
   social factors, 86
   psychological factors, 86
   increased social contact, 87–88
   in relation to genre-based approaches, 88–90
Acquisition
   genres, 88–90, 122
   speech acts, 49–50
   speaking skills, 92
   in relation to task-based teaching, 132
Activity theory, 105–107
   sociocultural theory, 105
   scaffolding, 105
   zone of proximal development, 105
   ecological perspective, 106
   learners' goals, 107
Adjunct courses, 88–90, 96
Affective objectives, 133, 141
Analytic syllabuses, 21–22, 103–104
Appenticeship, 88–90
Assessment of specific purpose language ability, 29, 146
Attention, 91, 139
Automaticization, 98
Autonomous functions of language education, 142
Authentic materials, 44, 81, 103–104, 114, 115, 116, 119, 152

Aviation English, 23, 49, 104, 136
Awareness raising activities, 115, 117 (*see also* Consciousness-raising activities)

B

Background knowledge, 25–26, 43, 137, 138, 146
Basic language, 17

C

Case method studies, 4, 125, 131, 132 (*see also* Projects)
CARS model (**C**reate **A R**esearch **S**pace), 56–57
Critical awareness, 5–6, 140–144, 146
   contrasted with pragmatic approaches, 140–141
   teaching activities, 141, 144
Critical needs analysis, 143–144
Comprehensible input, 116
Conciousness-raising activities, 115
Concordances, 63–67
   used in teaching, 67–68, 71, 122–123
Content-based instruction, 101–104 (*see also* Learning through content)
Controlled processing, 97–98
Common core, 15–17
Core vocabulary, 15–17, 35–38, 77–78
Cultural knowledge, 133, 138
Curricular innovation, 165

D

Data-driven approach, 9–10
Declarative knowledge, 98–99

CPSIA information can be obtained at www.ICGtesting.com
Printed in the USA
LVOW04s1153300814

401553LV00013B/403/P